BRITAIN'S STRATEGIC ROLE IN NATO

Also by George Richey

NATO'S STRATEGY: A Case of Outdated Priorities
(*with Patrick Cosgrave*)

Britain's Strategic Role in NATO

George Richey

Foreword by Gerald Frost
Director, Institute for European Defence and Strategic Studies

MACMILLAN
PRESS

First published 1986

Published by
THE MACMILLAN PRESS LTD
Houndmills, Basingstoke, Hampshire RG21 2XS
and London
Companies and representatives
throughout the world

Typeset by Latimer Trend & Company Ltd, Plymouth

Printed in Great Britain by
Anchor Brendon Ltd,
Tiptree, Essex

British Library Cataloguing in Publication Data
Richey, George
Britain's strategic role in NATO.
1. North Atlantic Treaty Organisation—
Great Britain
I. Title
355′.031′091821 UA646.5.G7
ISBN 0–333–42292–9

Contents

Foreword

Part of George Richey's virtue lies in his impatience and irritation with the obfuscation and evasions of politicians when they talk about defence. Like many with an interest in the subject he is aware that without a significant increase in the defence budget Britain will find it increasingly difficult to meet the full range of its commitments, and he laments the fact that few in public life are prepared to say this publically. He accepts that such an increase is quite unlikely to occur and therefore wishes to make sense of obligations which frequently tug in conflicting directions by recasting them in the light of changed circumstances rather than by further compromises.

As he points out, much has changed since the foundations of UK defence policy were laid in the postwar era. In particular, there has been the Soviet Union's rapid rise under two decades as a global maritime power, and the emergence of its Northern Fleet as the largest single concentration of naval power anywhere in the world. This, together with formidable Soviet land and air power in the region, constitues a threat to which he believes NATO has been slow to recognise. It should be answered, he believes, by a fundamental change in Britain's strategic posture. Accordingly, the British Army of the Rhine would be reduced in order to make resources available in the NATO Northern region. In addition to the creation of an 'assault' division, there would be an increase in naval strength in both submarines and surface ships, a development which would be in marked contrast to the recent trends in UK policy.

On this subject as on others, George Richey bases his recommendations on an unsentimental analysis of Britain's capabilities in relation to her resources and the threats which we are likely to face. It is not necessary to share all of his judgements about how these problems can be solved, or about the political consequences of particular options, in order to admire the clarity and vigour of his analyses. The problems and weaknesses in our defence arrangements to which he points have been neglected; in forcing us to acknowledge their existence and to think about how they may be dealt with he performs an invaluable public service.

GERALD FROST

Director
Institute for European Defence and Strategic Studies

Introduction

For some years now defence costs have risen out of all proportion to the increase in security which might have justified such increases. As weapons systems become more sophisticated not only does one get 'less bangs for the buck' but the skills required to operate and maintain these systems put strains on the defence establishment which has to compete with civilian firms who are only too willing to pay for highly skilled men and women with leadership qualities.

Great Britain's own role in the world has changed since 1945. Seen by her allies and foes alike as a Great Power and the leader of a worldwide Empire and Commonwealth she perceived herself in an imperial context. However, in historical terms in a relatively short time she has divested herself of all her major colonial commitments. As her worldwide military commitments reduced, particularly after the 1960s, so her role as a leading European NATO partner began to assume a greater importance. Nevertheless, some military commitments outside the NATO area remained and Britain's own military posture retained, in part, some of the capabilities which she had developed during her 'Imperial' role post-1945. One such capability is that of her nuclear forces.

However even though, in line with the worldwide reduction of commitments, and to a lesser extent a further reduction of her NATO responsibilities, for instance in the Mediterranean area, there is a case for maintaining that Britain is still taking on more than her fair share of the European defence burden.

It is the author's belief that, if Britain is to maintain a credible defence posture, hard decisions, many of which should have been taken years ago, must now be taken. To be effective in peace-time a national defence policy must be credible, if one is a member of an Alliance, to one's allies. It must be credible to the potential aggressor. However, equally important, it must have the general approval of the nation as a whole and this in the end means the electorate.

The 1983 General Election was possibly the first one in which not only was there a fundamental difference of approach over a national defence policy (the nuclear question) but defence was also a significant factor determining how electors eventually cast their votes. It is likely that this will still be so at the next General Election.

One problem when any subject of importance becomes a party

political matter is that 'Ya boo!' arguments tend to predominate. The aim of this book is to present a number of proposals, some of which will be highly controversial, which, so the author believes, need to be implemented if the UK is to maintain an effective defence policy.

To the reader who is a non-specialist in military matters, Chapter 2 has been included as an introduction to military tactics and part of the language of defence. It is hoped that by reading this chapter some of the problems faced by military commanders may come alive to the non-military reader.

GEORGE RICHEY

1 An Historical Perspective

PRE-1914

Britain is an island. Unlike political or military intentions, which can change overnight, this is an unchangeable fact. Events in the past have, of course, changed the way in which the British have perceived themselves and their relationship with others. In 1066 the old Saxon England was conquered by the Normans, themselves the descendants of the hardy, driving Norsemen from what is now Scandinavia. It was this which ensured that England would never be a political backwater in Europe but that her people, infected with the maritime adventurism of the Vikings, would have a major role to play in the destinies of the peoples of every continent in the world.

It meant too, that Britain would become a major political force in Europe and, during the course of the next nine hundred and seventeen years, would be the ally, or enemy, of virtually every country in Continental Europe.

The British, however, were and, at home still are, a small nation. Historically, because of her peculiarly British social structure, she has eschewed large standing armies. Whenever the British have had to fight, they have always done so with allies, and have frequently paid them as well, in order to get them into the field.

The great Duke of Marlborough commanded, not a British Army, although he was glad enough for the seasoning supplied by the small number of British infantry battalions, but an Allied Army. This practice of finding, or paying for, allies is a recurring theme throughout our history, possibly reaching its climax during the Napoleonic Wars. Thus the similarlity between the search for alliances against Spain, when she was the dominant force in Europe, then against the French and, in this century, against the German and Austro-Hungarian Empires, is so marked that one is justified in maintaining that this has been a cornerstone of British foreign and defence policy for centuries. Political conditions will never change sufficiently for this habit of seeking alliances in war and peace to become outdated or inappropriate.

However, along with this need there has developed a method of waging war which, in contrast to the European Continental powers, is peculiarly British. Because, since 1066, there has been no hostile army encamped within these islands, our wars have, in a sense, been remote from the people. Historically we have never liked standing armies and, even when eventually introduced, their size was severely restricted. Today this distaste, reinforced by the political folk memory of Cromwell and his ultimate use of force against Parliament, is reflected in the fact that the army needs to be legalised by Parliament each year whereas the navy does not.

The other side of this defence strategy coin is that Britain has structured her defence policy on control of the seas. Out of this came the great days of Empire when, within three centuries, this island's people and their descendants conquered four continents, introduced a new white population into two of them, North America and Australia, and gave to a third, India, three gifts which her previous rulers had never bestowed – a common language, an efficient communications system based on rail, and an effective Civil Service. Much the same can be said for Africa, incidentally, where again the use of English enables Africans, not only of different countries to communicate with each other but also those of different tribes within the same country to do so.

Within the context of an historical perspective the days of Empire might be considered to be an aberration even though it lasted for some three hundred years. Our military structure, particularly as it has affected the navy since, say, the mid-eighteenth century, was the result not so much because of our relationship with Europe but because of our world-wide Empire. That having been said, the role of the navy in the Napoleonic Wars was decisive, not in the ultimate defeat of Napoleon but in ensuring that he could never completely subjugate Continental Europe. This therefore gave us time. The campaigns in Egypt and Spain were classic examples, not of a continental but of a maritime strategy. A British Army could be re-embarked and redeployed elsewhere after the Battle of Corunna, as it was after Dunkirk, a century and a half later.

This habit of using other people to do our fighting for us extended to Empire. In India, the Bengal Army establishment in 1763 consisted of 1104 Britons and 9700 native Indian troops. Indeed the ability of the British successfully to raise sizeable forces from the local native populations, whilst providing the officers, has been quite remarkable.

But for this ability, it is likely that neither Indian nor African history would have been so closely bound up with Britain. Certainly the Indian Mutiny would not have been dealt with in the way it was, if the majority of Sepoys had not remained loyal to the Crown.

If it is true that in war Britain has always augmented her own regular forces with those of allies, then there is a strong case for saying that, as far as wars in Europe are concerned, the British method of the conduct of war has, in the main, been different from that of her Continental allies and foes. Every European nation has a folk memory of invasion. Even those long lasting neutrals, Sweden and Switzerland, have an active military history upon which to look back. The Central European powers, however, have known what 'a nation at arms' means. These powers have traditionally made use of large conscript armies. Napoleon and Bismarck each used the concept of a nation at war, and both Germany and France were experienced in the attrition rates, inevitable when large armies of conscripts are made to fight.

This experience was denied to the British. Even at Waterloo and the Crimea, the total effect on the civilian population was slight. True, some families suffered loss, but there was not the all pervading loss of young men which drained Germany during the Thirty Years War, or France during Napoleon's wars. Russia and Austria/Hungary also had large conscript armies which could be mobilised.

Peace in Europe in the past has all too often been a pause between conflict. Traditionally Britain's interests have been served by seeking to maintain the balance of power. This has usually been done by promoting alliances against the perceived threat to that balance of power. Britain's unique island position has meant that she has been able to maintain these alliances with the minimum commitment of land forces to the Continent. The Royal Navy not only allowed strategic flexibility within the alliances but also allowed Britain considerable flexibility as to with whom, and for how long, she would ally herself. Thus we find that, in 1815, German troops helped to turn tactical defeat of the French into certain rout, whilst a century later we had allied ourselves with France against Germany. When it suited us, we helped France against Spain, and Spain against France, and this help has been effective because of the use of sea power.

As we entered the twentieth century, the Central Powers, Germany and the Austro-Hungarian Empire, were becoming the dominant political, military and economic power in Europe. The balance was being upset. Even worse, Germany had begun to build a formidable navy. We sought allies. We looked to France, up till then our traditional enemy, and indeed even at that time our interests still clashed in the Middle East and Africa, and Russia, against whom we had fought in the Crimea. We made verbal, but not written, commitments involving the sending on an expeditionary force to the Continent. However, what we did not foresee was that the nature of war had already changed. For Britain, the traditional maritime strategy which had served the country so well, and indeed still was to do so, was to be augmented, for the first time, with 'a nation at war' policy. Despite the evidence, most leaders in Britain thought that a war in Europe would be short. True, the Prussian wars against both Austria and France, other than the Siege of Paris, had been over in weeks rather than months. However, another war had taken place, the American Civil War, the casualties of which, particularly for the South were horrendous. It was this war of which it could be said that it was the last of the old and the first of the modern wars. The effect of railways and trenches on the conduct of war were there for all to see. Few did.

In 1914, Britain sent an expeditionary force to France. It was an extremely well trained army and was to be augmented by the TA. However, the bulk of the British Army was the Indian Army and, as the war progressed, in line with our usual practice of producing allies, the White Dominions and India were to contribute tens of thousands to fight with us in France and elsewhere. In August 1914 the size of the Regular Army at home was 166000 men. On 5 August 1914, the House of Commons authorised its increase to 500000 men. There were also 250000 officers and men in the TA of whom some 17621 had undertaken to serve overseas under the General Service Obligation.

This small – 'contemptibly small' – British Army performed well. It stopped the German right hook and in doing so virtually sacrificed itself. However, it bought time. For the first time in history Britain was to deploy her citizenry in hundreds of thousands, to fight a war of attrition against the mass conscript armies of Central Europe. The Central Powers and France already knew, because they had experienced it, what continental war was all about. By January 1915 the strength of the BEF was 347384. The Citizen Army was being created. It was trained and armed, and then it went to France. In July 1916 what is now known as the Battle of the Somme began. From July to October 1916 the British suffered 453238 casualties. We had entered the big league.

POST-1919

By the end of the First World War, Britain had suffered over 700 000 dead and her Empire, the Dominions, India and other colonies, a further 200 000. The trauma on the political memory of the nation has remained. It is interesting to note that the invective poured on the memory of the British Senior Officer Corps' is not repeated in the same way in either France or Germany, both of whom suffered more than Britain. Being in Division One in the Continental War Game was not pleasant. After 1919 Britain quickly reverted to its traditional defence posture based on the Empire, overseas bases and the strengths of the Royal Navy and Indian Army.

Unfortunately the peace so hardly obtained in 1919 turned out to be a 20-year truce. Again we found ourselves faced with a militarily dominant Germany and once more we entered into commitments. This time 1940 differed from 1914. Whereas in 1914 the British Regular Army sacrificed itself for time, in 1940 the British Expeditionary Force successfully evacuated itself, together with an almost equal number of French troops, thus it was able to reassemble and re-equip itself. Time, on this occasion, was bought by the Channel. Britain once more reverted to a European War conducted on maritime lines.

In this respect events in Europe from 1941–4 were more akin to the operations conducted against Napoleon than those against the Kaiser. When eventually a British Army returned in strength to NW Europe, it was in conjunction with a strong ally. Not surprisingly casualties in the Second World War were never to reach the scale of those suffered in the Great War. However, a new factor had entered into military affairs. Air power had come of age. With air power had come the ability to project force over extremely long distances. Airborne forces could now present a formidable strategic threat as well as being able to be used to achieve tactical surprise. The nature of air power and its use have much in common with naval power. One could say that air power, unlike land (forces) power, is an extension of sea power. An effective maritime strategy depends as much on the correct use of air power as it does upon the use of sea power.

POST-1945

We must now concern ourselves with the events since 1945, for it is in this relatively short period that our traditional maritime strategy has been forced to give way to what is referred to as the 'Continental Strategy'. For the first time in our history, Britain has made a virtually permanent commitment to maintain an Army Corps, in fact some 35 per cent of the Regular Army, in Germany in peace-time. In the event of impending hostilities it will be under the Operational Command of a North Atlantic Treaty Organisation Officer, Commander Northern Army Group. It so happens that this officer is British. He in turn is under the operational command of a German officer holding the appointment, within NATO, of Commander-in-Chief Allied Forces Central Region (CINCENT). Besides the commitment of land forces, significant numbers of Royal Air Force units are also stationed in Germany and in the same way they come under operational control of a NATO Headquarters.

It is the aim of this book to see why this departure from our normal historical defence posture was made. To discuss in general whether the decisions taken in the late 1940s were justified and, if justified, what the factors were at the time which influenced the decision makers.

However, it is the author's view that whatever the justification in the 1940s, events have moved on so that, now, in the 1980s the situation is different. There is a need for a total review of Britain's defence commitments, not only in her own national interest but also in those of NATO. Some of the conclusions which will be presented will be controversial. It will be maintained though that the Defence Establishment and its political leadership has been guilty of inertia in planning. Changes are painful. Usually, however, they are painful in the military sphere because politicians have a habit of making political decisions affecting the services, without really considering the military implications; or, when those implications do become apparent, they then delay making corrective decisions until too late. The armed forces therefore tend to suffer both ways.

This is not to say that the services themselves are blameless. Decisions have been taken by the service chiefs which were quite clearly wrong and, what is more, known to be wrong. Inter-service argument and pigheadedness at high levels have resulted in years of delay in the introduction of new equipments which could have had disastrous results on our whole defence effort.

To give two examples; arguments over the original concept behind the introduction of the Short Take Off Vertical Landing (STOVL) carriers were first mooted in the 1960s. This concept needed a force of some six to eight ships to produce a viable force. That senior decision makers drove on with the introduction of CVA 01 and 02, both large aircraft carriers, made it inevitable that this particular programme would be cut. Nearly two decades later, the success or failure of the Falklands operations depended upon the single main shaft gearing of one ship, HMS *Hermes*. If the right decisions for the future of the Fleet Air Arm had been made in the 1960s, a Task Force with, say, four carriers would have been present and the early warning radar problem would, as part of the package, have been solved as well. Those who sent *Ark Royal* to the breaker's yard guaranteed the loss of every ship that went down to the Argentine Air Force, as, with her went the Gannet squadron, the long range early warning eyes and ears of the Fleet. The next example is given to show how pressures of political requirements to save money at no reduction in commitments have led to the introduction of militarily nonsensical solutions, themselves designed to hide a shortfall in savings or capabilities. In the late 1970s, the British Army of the Rhine (BAOR) divisions were ordered to be reorganised to produce a saving in manpower and money. Essentially the Brigade level of tactical command was eliminated. It so happened that at this time both the US and German armies had come to the conclusion that the most efficient divisional organisation was for there to be tactical commanders at brigade and battalion level with battalions being reduced in size but with more of them. The contrast to the British Army in Germany which was to reorganise with no brigades and with larger battalion commands was a source of considerable embarrassment to senior British officers in NATO appointments. 1st (British) Corps, the fighting formation of BAOR, was therefore for a time the only army formation in Europe on either side of the Iron Curtain with brigadeless divisions.

This reorganisation was known to be nonsense. No British Field Commander liked it and none, in private, thought it would work. Nevertheless, a small group of general officers in the Ministry of Defence forced it through, although, as a sop, it was said that the organisation would be 'introduced after trials'. The nature of these trials became clear when at question time at a senior officers' war course, one of the generals responsible for this extraordinary scheme, in reply to the question 'What if the trials show that the new organisation won't work', said 'It must be made to work'. So in the 1977 White Paper it was stated that 'Results of these trials have generally validated the reorganisation'. Sanity swiftly returned, for by the time the 1981 White Paper was produced we read 'We propose to reorganise the main regular structure of the Corps from the present four armoured divisions each of two brigades to three armoured divisions of three brigades'. Thus one of the shortest lived peace-time reorganisations was assigned to the dustbin of military nonsenses.

One thing that is needed within the services is absolute integrity. It is not good enough to produce a 'botch up' which will get by. Military capability can be measured and politicians must be faced honestly by the military as to the consequences of cuts. And, if cuts are to be made, then military commitments must go. If not, we face a possible military disaster.

In the nearly four decades since the end of the Second World War we have moved through a number of periods, each of about ten years, which is characterised by a major decision of strategic importance or by a significant change in the political or military structures of the time.

1945–55

Immediately after the Second World War, the Western Powers demobilised. They were faced with a prostrate Germany now divided and an exhausted Europe. The Red Army had for the first time arrived into Central Europe and, unlike those of the allies, retained its manpower. So ominous was the political situation that National Service was reintroduced in 1947. Not only were we faced with the task of occupying Germany; but this occupation began to take on a possible defence task of Western Europe against a Soviet Russian threat of monumental proportions at least in terms of numbers. At the same time internal security commitments in Palestine and Greece were British responsibilities. The twelve-year anti-terrorist Malayan War started in 1948 and in 1952 civil unrest started in Kenya. A full decade indeed, in which the army in particular was heavily committed.

A mutual defence pact, the Brussels Treaty, was signed in 1948, to be replaced by the North Atlantic Treaty Organisation (NATO) created in 1949. For the first time in history, in peace-time, a British Army was committed to mainland Europe. This commitment was made, in part, to persuade the Americans that the British and Europeans were serious about their security and that they, the Americans, should commit themselves in a like manner to Western Europe. The conventional military threat from Russia was formidable, but the United States had the atomic bomb. Thus grew up the strategy of immediate nuclear retaliation, with land forces having the 'tripwire' role. They were, so to speak, the trigger which, if pressed by an aggressor, would set off the nuclear response.

1955–65

The decade of Suez, the development of a Soviet Russian nuclear capability and the Cuban missile crisis. An important British defence landmark was the 1957 White Paper. This, written in the days of undoubted US and NATO nuclear superiority, proposed the ending of national service within three years. Once National Service ended, Britain, alone of the European NATO and Warsaw Pact (WP) countries, would, in time, cease to have a reservoir of trained and semi-trained men. There would be few reserves, and yet the commitment to keeping an army in Germany remained. During this time the 'commando ship' concept was developed by the Royal Navy and by 1961 the Amphibious Task Group, consisting of fixed wing carriers, commando carriers, other specialised amphibious shipping as well as support ships, was an established part of the fleet. Successful commando deployments were carried out in Jordan (1958) and Kuwait (1961). The closure of the Suez Canal put an extra strain on Britain's military resources, as, since India and Pakistan had become independent, more British, as against Commonwealth, troops had to be deployed East of Suez. It was towards the end of this decade that inter-service rivalry for fewer resources began to become rather serious. Essentially the future of the Fleet Air Arm was being questioned, particularly by the Royal Air Force, who proposed their 'island base strategy' and the use of air refuelling.

1965–75

Having learnt its lesson from the Cuban missile crisis, Russia had begun to develop a maritime strategy of its own and a fleet to go with it. The nature of the strategic threat posed by Russia began to change fundamentally. She was producing a modern 'blue water' fleet which now equals that of the United States in most areas, and is ahead in submarines, it is only observably inferior in the field of strike carriers. At the same time she was achieving nuclear parity with the USA. Her ground forces which for years had been regarded as large, but not too well equipped and inflexibly led, were now becoming ominously well equipped, particularly in tanks and artillery. There were signs that the Red Army leaders were also aware of their own stereotype training shortcomings. NATO's own immediate nuclear response strategy had now begun to look less credible to NATO, and probably also to the Warsaw Pact. Thus the so-called 'flexible response strategy' was developed. This implied a period of non-nuclear operations, in other words instead of buying time with ground (this early non nuclear conflict was referred to as the aggressive delaying battle) it was now proposed to buy time with blood (the initial battle would presumably be more aggressive than delaying). The significance of this change of strategic concept upon the small all-Regular British Army which was in Germany went unremarked, but, by the early 1970s, the fact was that because there were no large numbers of reservists to replace casualties as there had been in the 1940s and 1950s, the implications if deterrence should fail were obvious and grave.

1975–85

NATO's defence strategy had already undergone modification and, not only was there a 'flexible response' strategy, but in the Central Front, essentially West Germany, there was by this time, at the determined insistence of the Germans, a forward defence posture. The nuclear balance had in the meantime tipped in Soviet Russia's favour with development of the SS20s. The Red Navy had now received its own Short Take-Off Vertical Landing (STOVL) carriers and, with its equipments of electronics and weaponry, posed a serious threat to NATO.

The discovery and exploitation of North Sea oil by Norway and Britain gave a strategic significance to the Northern Region of NATO which was certainly not apparent in the 1940s and 1950s. Unfortunately, this appears to have had no significant effect on either Britain's or NATO's strategic defence planning.

Throughout this time the UK developed and deployed its own independently controlled strategic nuclear deterrent force. Initially this was the responsibility of the Royal Air Force but subsequently passed to the Royal Navy with its fleet of Polaris equipped submarines. It is now planned that Polaris will be replaced by Trident, another submarine-based system.

2 Definitions, Organisation, Tactics

A major problem facing any writer on defence is that he uses words which to the serviceman are the stuff of his everyday job. The layman may well have some notions as to the form of war, but it is unlikely that he can easily visualise, say, an armoured division deployed or the problems facing commanders and staffs in moving that same division, at short notice, to another location, possibly seventy miles away.

The immense difficulties facing a naval task force in trying to locate a submarine, despite all the advanced technology in Anti-submarine (AS) warfare, can only be imagined and even servicemen may get a false impression from training. That an interceptor fighter aircraft has characteristics about it that make it unsuitable as a ground attack aircraft is something which has to be borne in mind when 'playing the numbers game' in assessing the relative strengths of opposing air forces.

Words, again used by the military strategist and serviceman, have particular meanings within the context of defence and have to be used in the context of their precise meaning. As far as possible this meaning will be explained on the first occasion such a word is used, unless the text makes its meaning absolutely clear. However, it was considered useful for the book to contain a number of definitions, as well as an introduction to some military tactics. In this way it is intended, first, to ensure that the reader does not have to frequently rush to a military dictionary and, secondly, that with a background of the 'nuts and bolts' of military tactics and the problems facing commanders in combat the reader is able to follow strategic arguments upon which some of the more controversial proposals are based.

NUCLEAR FORCES

Strategic nuclear forces are those capable of striking at military targets, governmental centres, industrial facilities and populated areas in an adversary's homeland, or those weapons systems deployed to defend against such strikes. These can be further subdivided into global (intercontinental) strategic forces and regional strategic forces, that is those of shorter range or more limited deployment.[1]

This implies that nuclear forces deployed in the US with the task of striking at targets in the USSR are strategic; however, some weapon systems deployed in Europe may also be regarded as strategic.

Tactical nuclear forces are those nuclear-armed elements of sea, land and air forces which are primarily designed and intended for deployment against military targets in a theatre of operations, such as Central Europe.[1]

The problem with these definitions is that of deciding, if ever a nuclear weapon was fired in anger, whether it was tactical or strategic. Escalation is one of the most likely outcomes if ever a nuclear weapon is fired. For instance, would the Soviet High Command accept a 'low yield' (the term used to express the power of a nuclear weapon) weapon exploded on a second echelon formation some 400–600 miles from the front as tactical or strategic? What if a high yield weapon is fired on a leading Warsaw Pact division? In other words, which might be the more important factor in Russian eyes, yield or location? Or is the initial delivery point significant? An aircraft taking off from the UK and releasing a weapon in East Germany might be regarded as strategic, whereas, if it had started its mission from West Germany, could it be said to be tactical? Certainly the Russians have made it clear that any nuclear strike on their own territory will be regarded as if it had been fired from the United States. This suggests that it is where the device is exploded that is important. However, the West Germans might equally maintain that any weapon fired onto their territory, whether or not it was from a Warsaw Pact (WP) unit actually deployed at the time in West Germany (the assumption here being that there has been a period of non-nuclear combat in the Central Region with WP tactical success), will be regarded as having been fired by the USSR. What does come out of all this, is the extraordinary difficulties inherent in the nuclear question. Certainly there are no easy solutions.

The delivery means of nuclear weapons are of three sorts, aircraft, missile and gun. Aircraft can be armed with free-fall bombs or missiles. Missiles can also be launched from the ground or from under the ground (normally from hardened silos), or from under the sea. They may be guided or Free Flight Rockets (FFR). Missiles may have single or multiple warheads. These warheads themselves may be separately targeted and have terminal guidance, that is they can be given 'corrections' in the last phase of flight to put them on to their target. Shells are free-flight projectiles, have limited range but are very accurate.

Although not comprehensive, the following are some definitions of terms that will be used in the book:[2]

ICBM Intercontinental ballistic missile.

IRBM Intermediate range ballistic missile (ranges of about 3000 km fall into this category).

SRBM Short range ballistic missile (most weapons in this category have ranges of less than 500 km, exception is Pershing 1A with a range of 720 km).

SLBM Sea launched ballistic missile.

MIRV Multiple independently targeted re-entry vehicle. Each warhead can be directed towards an individually selected target. The warheads are mounted on a 'bus' which is guided through a series of predetermined velocity changes, releasing a warhead after each change.

Cruise missile A non-ballistic air-breathing missile using sophisticated guidance systems, it can be (a) GLCM Ground launched Cruise missile, (b) ALCM Air launched Cruise missile, (c) SLCM Sea (or submarine) launched Cruise missile.

ABM Antiballistic missile. A missile system specifically designed to detect, intercept and destroy incoming nuclear warheads.

SRAM Short range attack missiles (air launched missiles).

Strike An attack by nuclear weapon(s).

Strike (aircraft) An aircraft specifically designed for delivering nuclear weapons, or one armed with nuclear weapons (many aircraft are dual role, that is they can be attack or strike aircraft).

First strike capability The ability to destroy all, or nearly all, of the enemy's strategic nuclear forces in a pre-emptive nuclear attack. (It is doubtful, now that submarine based missiles are deployed by both West and East whether a first strike capability can ever exist again.)

Second strike capability The ability to mount a nuclear attack after a first strike. For a strategy of deterrence the opponent must be convinced of the reality of this capability, so that a pre-emptive first strike ceases to be a realistic option.

SALT I The series of negotiations beginning in the late 1960s resulting in the 'Interim Agreement' between the United States and the USSR on Certain Measures with Respect to the Limitation of Strategic Offensive Arms' and the 'Treaty between the USA and the USSR on the limitations of Anti-Ballistic Missile Systems' signed in Moscow on 25 May 1972.

SALT II The negotiations since SALT I culminating in the signing on 18 June 1979 in Vienna of the 'Treaty between the USSR and the USA on the Limitations of Strategic Offensive Arms' and the 'Protocol to the Treaty Between the USSR and the USA on the Limitations of Strategic Offensive Arms'. When the Soviets invaded Afghanistan in December 1979, President Carter suspended the SALT II Agreement from Senate Ratification.

NON-NUCLEAR FORCES

Land forces are those forces which fight on the ground. Having said that many armies will have, as well as tanks, artillery, armoured personnel carriers (APCs) and so forth, helicopters and other light aircraft; some may even have ships. However, army, aircraft and ships are severely limited in their tactical role and performance.

The basic fighting formation of the army is the division. It is at this level that all the elements, both combat and logistic, of warfare are found under a single commander. There are varieties of division each tailored to fit a particular role:

Tank (or armoured) division A tank oriented organisation whose role is offensive. It is this type of division which would be used to exploit a break through, or would be used by the defence as a powerful mobile counter-attack formation.

Mechanised (or motorised) division A division with a more even distribution of tank units to infantry units. This type of division is suitable for leading an advance as the tank/infantry ratio gives more flexibility to a commander.

Artillery division A supporting division enabling a senior commander to reinforce his forward divisions with more, and heavier, artillery according to his tactical plan.

Airborne (or airportable) division An infantry division equipped on 'light scales'. It is delivered into or near to the combat area by air. These formations usually have a limited endurance without reinforcement or support from other formations.

Supporting troops, logistic units, 3rd and 4th line transport These types of unit will be found at all levels. However, many of these units will be in the rear areas and under 'army' or 'army group' control.

The organisation of the various armies differs slightly from country to country. Some of the names of formations differ between NATO and the WP so it is not feasible to produce a standard formation. Although the actual numbers are not absolutely accurate to any one NATO army, the organisation chart (Figure 2.1) will at least give an idea as to the size and capability of land force units and formations.

These organisation charts do not exactly match any particular national organisation. However, they will give an idea as to the size and weight of fire power that any level of formation or unit has available to its Field Commander.

An armoured division (of 2 Tank bdes and 1 Mec bde) on the move will have to co-ordinate the movement of something of the order of:

200 tanks (including battle tanks, recovery tanks, artillery observation post tanks and command tanks).
100 guns (including field, heavy and air defence artillery).
700 plus armoured personnel carriers (APCs) (including infantry APC, command, recovery, medical, artillery, anti-tank, artillery command APC).

as well as nearly 1000 lorries with ammunition, petrol and other stores needed to keep the division fighting.

This is a formidable task for a staff in peace-time. In war, such a move will require:

(a) Reconnaissance (Recce) of the route – repair of bridges, the planning of detours.
(b) An air defence system will have to be deployed to protect the division on the move.
(c) Timings of the move and co-ordination with other user formations will be vital.
(d) Recce of the reception area or battle area if the division is moving into combat will have to be carried out.

If the air situation is adverse, it is likely that the move will have to be done at night or, if done in the day, by tactical moves from hide to hide. Damage to the route and to units by enemy action will have to

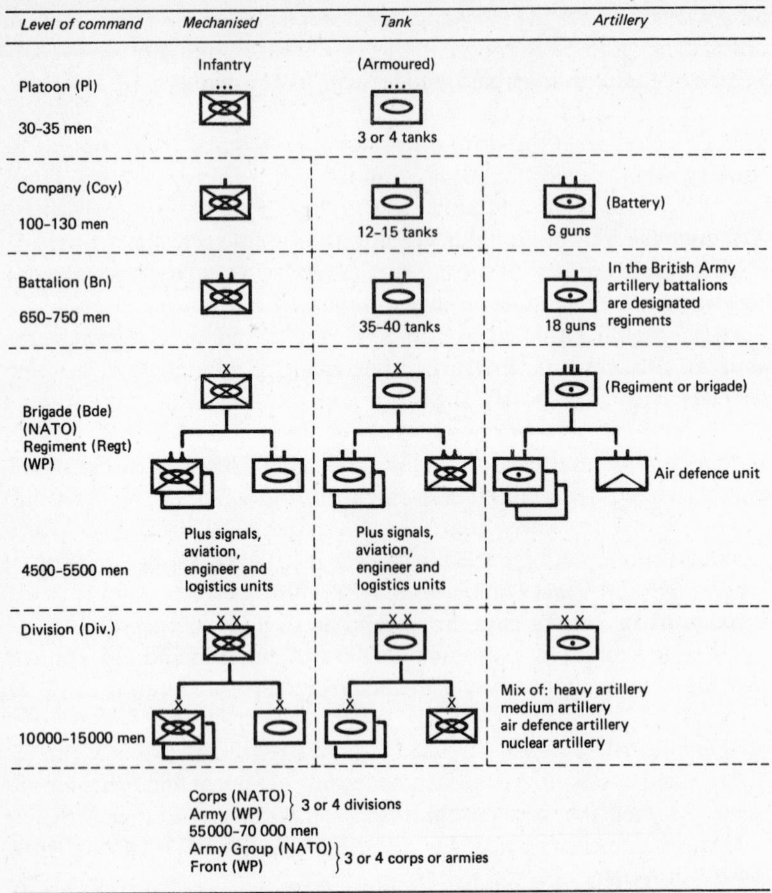

Figure 2.1 *Note:* The boxes are the normal military conventional signs used to denote military units and will be used later in the book.

be planned for, so that the whole move does not grind to a halt. A well trained division is a pleasure to watch. One that is ill-trained or inexperienced can very easily get things badly wrong.

The Attack

WP doctrine uses movement, shock and continuous fighting throughout a 24-hour day to overcome the defence. Over a front, possibly up to four break-through areas will have been planned. The task of the leading echelons (1st Tactical Echelon) will be to identify, engage and overrun the forward defensive positions. The 2nd Tactical Echelon will be used to reinforce or fight through exhausted units or, if there has been an initial success, to exploit the break-through. Once a break-through has been achieved the second strategic echelon will be committed to the major exploitation.

Throughout the early phases of the battle, tactical ground attack aircraft will be used to recce and attack artillery positions, reserve formations and known choke points (vital bridges, routes in valleys). Because the effectiveness of the defence will depend upon the timely move of the reserves, as well as trying to locate those units, the WP will be subjecting the NATO tactical command radio nets to an intense barrage of electronic warfare (EW) such as jamming in order to stop command decisions being converted into received orders.

Chemical warfare (CB) is regarded as a normal means of non-nuclear combat by the WP, thus area attacks with CB agents can be expected on selected units. The effect of CB on the defence will, no matter how effective the protective clothing, be significant after a relatively short time. The fact is that the fighting efficiency of a man dressed in his 'Noddy suit' drops markedly after a few hours. In this respect there will be ample scope for real and false chemical attacks. All this will add to the general confusion of battle, well described in the telling phrase 'the fog of war'.

A WP division will advance against the defence led by its recce units. These will be operating a couple of miles ahead of the leading elements of the division, the advance guard. Their mission is to locate the defenders, push round defended locations if possible, or if this is not possible, to identify the location and strength of the defences for the advance guard. The aim of the advance guards, and on a divisional front there might be two, each on its own axis, will be to 'bounce' the forward defended positions if possible. If not, it will pin down the enemy and form the platform from which a regimental level attack can be mounted (Figure 2.3). The main body of the division would hope to 'pass through' and continue the advance (Figure 2.4). Timings are difficult to gauge but with a well trained formation that finds itself having to fight through the forward defence, possible timings may be as follows:

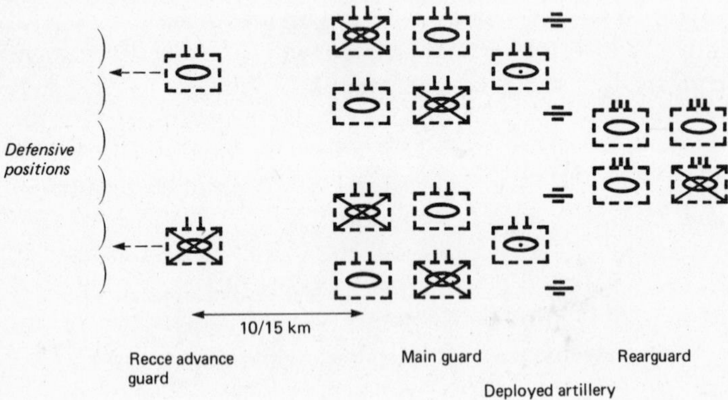

Figure 2.2 Advance to contact

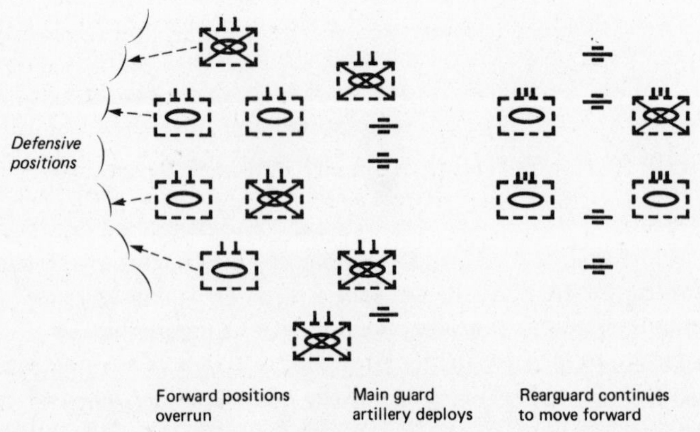

Figure 2.3 Advance guard attacks

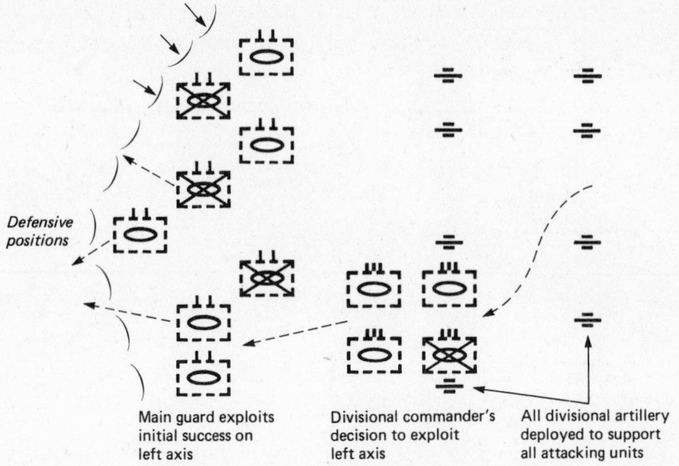

Figure 2.4 Main guard attacks

Zero	The time at which contact is made by forward recce units.
Zero to +1 hour	Recce units establish that they have come up against main forward defence (Figure 2.2).
+1 to $+2\frac{1}{2}$ hours	Advance guard advances to contact and mounts co-ordinated battalion sized attack – which fails.
$+2\frac{1}{2}$ to $+6\frac{1}{2}$ hours	Main guard advances to contact and mounts co-ordinated regimental attack with full supporting artillery (Figure 2.4).
$+6\frac{1}{2}$ to +10 hours	Reserve regiment prepared to exploit or take part in divisional attack (Figure 2.5).

What the attackers will try to avoid is failure of the initial co-ordinated attacks. It is therefore likely that, if the defenders can hold against the advance guard, a pause will be forced, as the next attack will require careful preparation. Even with large numbers of tanks, attacks are no longer glorious cavalry charges. An attack by an armoured formation has to be carefully planned, and orchestrated.

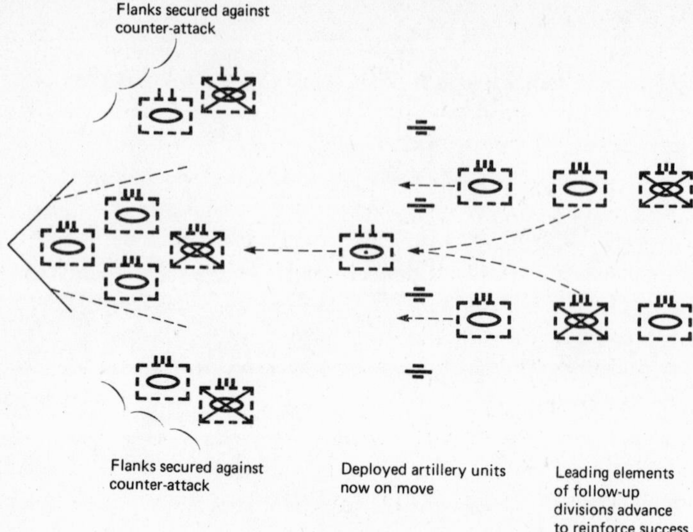

Figure 2.5 Exploitation

The artillery fire plan must be prepared and this will require ranging onto the targets, the passing of technical firing data to the participating batteries which, in the meantime, will be surveying in their guns. Recce parties will go forward to view the ground. Orders will need to be given down to each unit and sub-unit. All this takes time because, if things are rushed, the attack is likely to fail.

At army and front level the attacking commanders will be more interested in the location and possible movement of the defending reserve divisions. They will be keen to find and destroy HQs and nuclear units. If airborne forces have been allocated to them, they will be using these not only as a strategic threat (the possible use of airborne forces is a major problem for a defending commander as he must be prepared to use units to secure the rear areas), but when they are committed this will be in an area or against a target which will be of most use to him (for example, a vital bridge – which if secured before it is blown could affect the course of the battle).

The Defence

Despite the advantages that the attacker has, he knows for instance when and where he intends to advance, the defender does have a number of factors in his favour. He can select his own ground; he can thoroughly recce it; he can, if he has time, add to the natural strength of the position by the use of minefields and other obstacles. His artillery will have been surveyed in so that all batteries can use the ranging data of the others, thus enabling the accurate concentrated fire of many units to be brought down on any one target. The most effective use of artillery is for many guns to fire a few rounds together at one target rather than a few guns firing more rounds each over a longer period of time. Anti-tank weapons can be sited in *en filade* so that not only will they be unobserved from the front but they can hit at tanks side-on rather than front-on. In the NATO context, commanders at all levels can, in peace-time, familiarise themselves with the ground in their planned areas of responsibility. Contingencies can be rehearsed, both on cloth models and on the actual ground.

The aim of the defence is to stop the enemy. He can do this by a number of means almost certainly in combination:

(a) Holding naturally strong positions.
(b) By manœuvre, enticing the attackers into 'killing' areas.
(c) By well timed concentrated counter-attacks.
(d) By the judicious use of air power, stop or severely slow down the reserve units of the leading divisions and the leading units of the reserve divisions. This will deprive the attacker of the capability of exploitation if his initial attacks are successful. The air commanders, as do the land commanders, will carefully recce likely choke points where air attacks will be most effective.

In essence the defence has a layout similar to the order of march of the attacker. In front of the forward held positions will be a highly mobile covering force. Its aim is to identify the main axis of advance. It will do this by forcing the attacking recce units to fight for information. Indeed, a skilful covering force may well force the advance guard to deploy. This buys time. Eventually, however, the covering force will be forced to withdraw through the forward defensive locations, when it will probably be given another role. But the chances are that it will need rest because, if it has done its job well, it will be below strength (Figure 2.6).

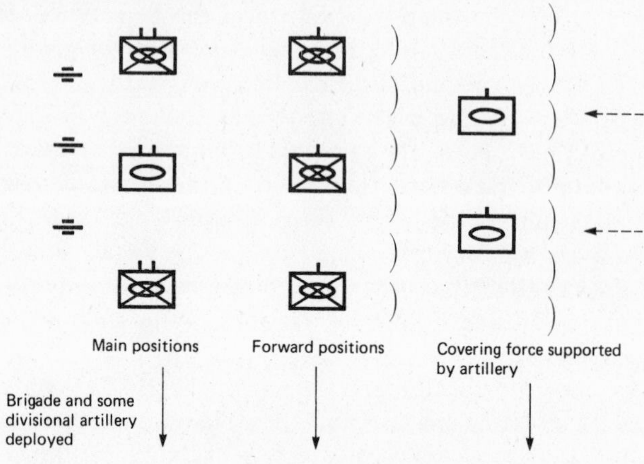

Figure 2.6 Initial contact

The forward positions, carefully chosen for the good fire and observation they afford, should be able to hold anything less than a co-ordinated major attack.

Observed artillery and long-range anti-tank weapons will take their toll of the enemy long before he approaches close to the defended locations. However, at some point the defence is going to have to withstand major attacks. In the diagrams of the attack we postulated two in that particular division, which would be faced, let us assume, by a brigade of two mechanised battalions and one tank battalion, supported by an artillery battalion with extra divisional artillery on call (Figure 2.7).

Behind the forward positions are the main positions, which in this particular case have been laid out in order to invite initial success, so that the divisional counter-attack (which will be carried out by the armoured brigade) can destroy the main elements of the attacking division (Figure 2.8).

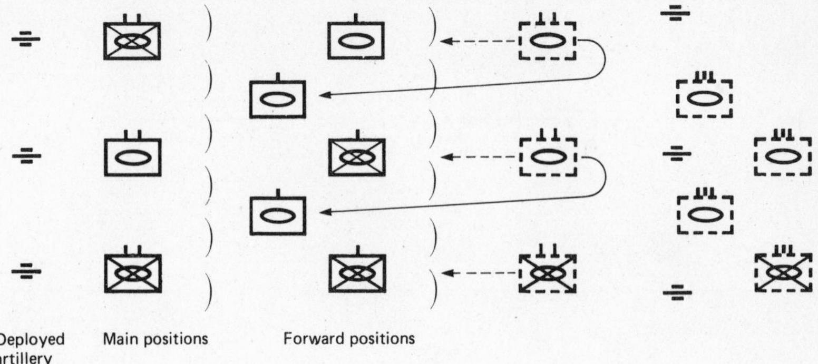

Figure 2.7 Covering force withdraws

The forward positions are held as long as possible, then a co-ordinated realignment is made linking the forward units with the main positions. This will have been preplanned and rehearsed. When the expected main guard attack develops the attackers will therefore advance into a piece of ground which (conveniently) is dominated by a feature to the West. Once the enemy has committed himself to this position the counter-attack co-ordinated by division will be launched (Figure 2.9).

At this stage, the battle will be decided by morale, training, luck and generalship. As far as the defence is concerned it is buying time. Time is bought by giving away ground, or, as every commander and soldier in NATO must know, by blood. In this scenario we suggest that it will be the latter.

The diagrammatic presentation of a brigade level defence postulates in this particular case one way that a divisional counter-attack might have been preplanned. Many situations, because of the nature of the ground, might require a different defensive layout and concept.

However, what is common to all defensive plans is the vital importance of the command decision as to where and when to commit the reserve. An attacker is most vulnerable to counter-attack at the moment that he has achieved initial success, in, say, taking a defended position, and before he has consolidated by bringing forward his own follow-up units.

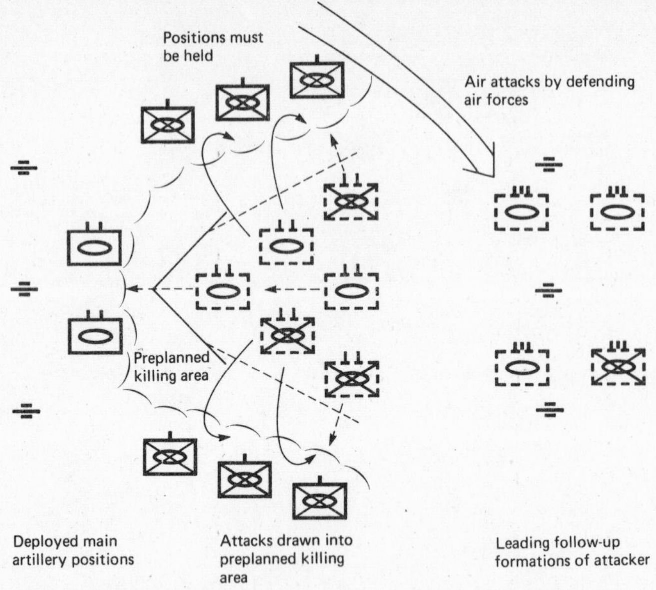

Figure 2.8 Planned manoeuvre by forward defending units

Defending commanders at each level will plan to take advantage of this by having preplanned and, ideally, rehearsed counter-attacks. One of the main lessons of combat repeatedly relearned is that determined well co-ordinated counter-attacks, even by relatively small forces, can have a local success out of all proportion to their numbers. In the defence diagrammatically shown, the counter-attack is shown being carried out by a brigade. It would therefore be the divisional commander's decision. Behind him is the corps commander and it will be his decision to commit the corps reserve, probably an armoured division. At the next level of command, army group, there should be a reserve of corps size. Unfortunately in the Central Region of NATO, Germany, there are not sufficient forces to produce meaningful reserves at all levels of command. Within the context of the land battle if ever fought in the Central Region it is not

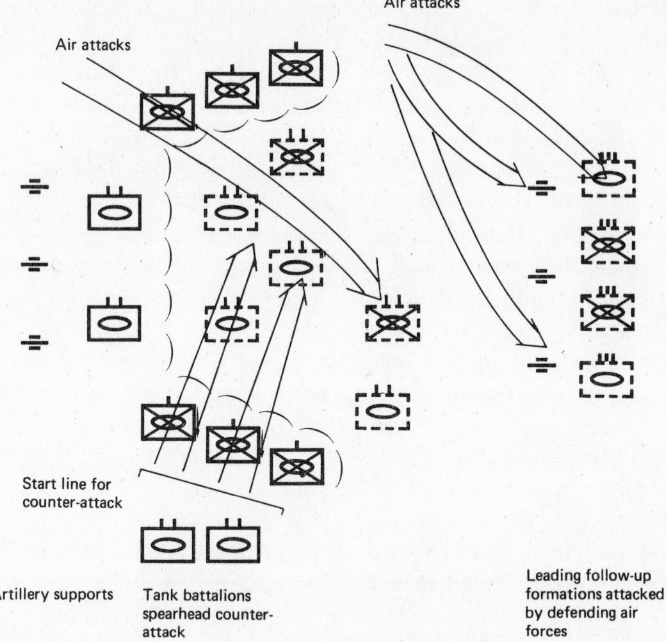

Figure 2.9 Divisional counter stroke

overstating the case to say that the decisions to commit the NATO reserve divisions are those which will determine the outcome of the non-nuclear battle.

The need therefore for commanders at each level to receive timely and accurate information as to what is actually happening is vital. Much of this will come from air force sources and this underlines the vital importance of good and realistic training in peace-time. An understanding on the part of airmen as to how ground forces operate is essential therefore whilst land force commanders and staffs must be careful not to waste scarce air resources by requiring unrealistic performances from them.

Air Forces

Air power has an inherent flexibility denied to the soldier. Its power can be projected over great distances and can be concentrated, thus command and co-ordination of air forces is better kept at the highest possible level. This in contrast to land forces, where commanders at each level are given the resources with which to carry out their missions. Aircraft are expensive. Many of their weapons are specialised which requires very careful preplanning so that the right 'mix' of weaponry is readily available to the air commander.

The air commanders have to weigh up conflicting missions. A major factor will be the activities of the opposing air forces and, although air superiority in the old sense is probably not on, nevertheless most army commanders would agree that the main task of NATO's air will be to keep the WP air off their backs. This will be done by engaging in aerial combat and taking out the WP forward air fields.

The air battle over the forward battle area (FBA) is complicated because the army has its own air defence weapons, both for point and area defence. NATO cannot afford to engage its own aircraft successfully.

The air commander will be keen to ensure that his own aircraft returning from missions well beyond the forward edge of the battle area (FEBA) are not shot down by the NATO ground forces. Land forces on the other hand will not want their own weapon systems restricted. Once soldiers have been subjected to air attack there is a marked inclination to fire at any low flying aircraft coming from the enemy's direction. Here good co-ordination and mutual confidence born of an effective peace-time training programme is essential.

The second battle with which the air commanders will be concerned is the land battle, for if this is lost, regardless of what has gone on in the air, the war is lost. They need, in peace-time, to develop the techniques of target acquisition and data handling, so that they are able to take timely decisions, to ensure that adequate and accurate fire power is directed at critical targets in the close battle area. The relative priorities betweeen army targets in the immediate battle (those targets which will affect the tactical battle within the next hour or so), targets of attrition (reserve units, for instance, which may join the battle in the next 10–24 hours), and their own air battle targets whether counter-air or interdiction against airfields must be decided.

One major problem facing the air commanders is the maintenance of their own nuclear capability. Many of their aircraft are dual purpose, in the sense that they can be used on conventional attack missions as well as on strike missions. Every dual purpose aircraft lost in the non-nuclear battle (the expression 'phase' is not used, as this would suggest a pre-planned time at which nuclear weapons would be used), means one aircraft less available should it be necessary to fight a nuclear battle. Of course the less aircraft used to support the land battle, the more likely, and earlier, will be the request for 'release' (this is the word to denote the political authority to fire nuclear weapons). In the heat of battle the pressures that will be exerted on the air commanders particularly by hard pressed land force commanders, will be enormous. They will need cool heads but above all they will require good and timely intelligence not only about their own air battle but also about the land battle. It is an interesting paradox that, because of the way in which air forces can react to a battle situation, a senior air commander needs to know information about the land battle well before his land force opposite number. Tactical decisions in the air environment are taken at a high level; those in the army are taken at each level of command. A general only takes a decision after each level of command has done its bit. These decisions therefore do not have immediate effect because of the delays inherent in the transmission and carrying out of orders. The air commander, on the other hand, can produce immediate and devastating power to influence a particular tactical situation. He also has the unenviable knowledge that he, unlike his army equivalent, can lose, in a very short time, the major element of his fire-power if he makes an unwise decision.

The difference in command style is very marked between air and land forces. Air resources have to be co-ordinated at a very high level of command. It can even be that an air commander will specify the weapons load to be carried and the number of aircraft to be allotted to a particular mission. He has to keep a very tight hold on his resources. The land commander, on the other hand, will allocate resources to his junior commanders so that they are able to carry out his orders. How they do so is up to them. Neither way is wrong, each is suited to the particular service. However, sometimes the reasons for these different styles are not always appreciated which is one of the reasons that establishments such as the Joint Services Staff College and Joint Warfare Establishment existed. Alas these have been abolished as part of cost saving exercises. Paradoxically within a couple of years of these two decisions the forces of the Crown found themselves involved in a major joint warfare operation in the South Atlantic.

Naval Forces

The command and control of naval forces is similar to that of air forces in that decisions are taken at a high level. Navies operate on the 'task force' concept. A task force is a group of ships specifically brought together, for a particular task under a single Task Force Commander. This commander can be directly under the operational command or control of the Fleet Commander at Northwood (in the case of the UK) or Supreme Allied Commander Atlantic Saclant (in the case of NATO) whose headquarters is at Norfolk, Virginia or, of course, one of the intermediate HQs at lower levels of NATO command.

Although many naval vessels are specialist, most are able to carry out more than one function. Destroyers and frigates, for instance, have a quick firing gun which can be used in giving naval gunfire support (NGS) to land forces. There are specialist amphibious warfare ships ranging from the command facility ship such as *Fearless*, to the light carriers, the latest of which are supposed to be AS carriers but these can also, as was demonstrated in the Falklands campaign, carry troops and/or Harrier aircraft and perform a very different role.

Successful naval operations are a matter of teamwork. No one ship can do everything. A task force must therefore be constituted so that enemy forces can be engaged well before they are able to inflict damage to units of the force. Ideally the fleet carrier will form the basis of a 'blue water' navy as it is the carrier that, with its embarked air squadrons, provides the long distance early warning so vitally needed in modern war. The attack carrier is able to project its own fire power well beyond the range of any other ship or submarine. However, it needs its escort of AS ships and air defence (AD) frigates.

AS warfare is a matter of teamwork. The oceans are large. Ocean going attack and ballistic missile carrying submarines are able to operate for weeks underwater. A skilful submarine commander can hide successfully by making use of the cold layers in the sea, these can distort the echoes from the sonar equipment. He can also use silent drills to avoid detection.

Passive receivers have been placed around the oceans so that a continuous record of all ships and boats passing over or near them is kept. Each vessel has its own noise 'signature' and a skilled operator can even name ships from their recorded noises. Other receivers are towed by ships, lowered into the water by helicopters or dropped from long range maritime recce aircraft (Nimrod is an example), so a submarine commander may be unaware that he is being tracked.

Unlike land operations where the traditional view is that to win the attacker needs to have a 3:1 majority over the defence, in naval warfare the opposite is true. A defending navy requires to outnumber the aggressor's hulls. Indeed, the problem of numbers in this respect is similar to that faced by land force commanders in internal security operations. The trouble is that a navy which has the task of maintaining the security of the seas must deploy everywhere.

The attacker, on the other hand, can concentrate his forces at his own time, at the place of his choosing and he can achieve local superiority relatively easily, unless the sea denial force has early intelligence of the aggressor's initial movements. The world's choke points, those specific seas, mainly straits, through which significant traffic passes are well known. They cannot all be secured by NATO forces, as most are well outside NATO's formal boundaries. Yet the denial of a passage thousands of miles from Europe could be vital to the European NATO countries. Over 80 per cent of all the world's trade is still ship-borne, and the bulk of that most strategically vital commodity, oil, is either transported by ship, or is extracted from the sea bottom.

Sea power, unlike air or land power, can be used as a form of military or diplomatic pressure in a way that enables the maritime power to graduate its pressure at will. It can be maintained for long periods of time and the pressure graduated to a higher or lower level as the political situation demands.

Logistics plays a vital role in naval planning, as it does for all military services. However, in the case of the navy, the consumption of oil is considerable. If a naval force is on station for a reasonable period, a surprisingly large fleet supply train needs to be set up. Resupply by sea (RAS) produces strategic and tactical problems not normally faced by air force commanders, who may well have others such as inter-operability, and armies can sometimes live off the land (or their enemy if they win).

In summary, naval and air forces operate with a considerable degree of control at a high level and both have developed the communications to back up this command concept. In contrast, of the sum total of tactical decisions taken within the land battle, most are at a low level. Personal responsibility for immediate tactical decisions in the navy and air force is not, as a rule, assumed below officer rank (the pilot of a fighter is an officer as is the ship's captain). At battalion level many immediate tactical decisions will be taken by NCOs. Command decisions are more easily translated into received orders in sea and air warfare. When a captain of a ship orders 'port 60 degrees', the ship and everyone in it proceeds on the new bearing. If a battalion commander wishes to change his unit's movements, every single individual soldier must get the word, and they will not all have radios. In the heat of battle even that which appears very simple will not in practice be all that easy. The point is that no matter how good the training, no matter how well co-ordinated the pre-battle briefings, the fact of the matter is 'no plan survives contact'. This is where good training takes over.

3 The Threat

Foreign and defence policies will normally run on similar lines. A foreign policy which takes no account of strategic realities is not, in the end, likely to prove effective. A defence policy pursued as an end in itself will not only be wasteful but positively dangerous. Clearly, before any rational defence policy can be formulated, the likely threat or threats must be identified. Priorities will have to be set and, ultimately, funds allocated to the defence planners sufficient for the minimum practical capabilities to be produced to meet the potential military requirements.

Unfortunately, life is not that simple. A prime threat in terms of the overall strategic position to Britain and its allies will obviously have the major influence on long-term defence planning. However, in the last twelve years, the main real, as opposed to anticipated, tasks which have engaged British forces were both unforeseen, Northern Ireland and the Falklands campaign. Both these operations required forces armed and equipped for a type of military activity at variance with the present major role occupying the army, namely an armoured threat projected against the North German Plain.

What then is this threat? Is Soviet Russia really the major threat? And if it is thought to be, ought it to be? These are important questions, for unless the answers derived therefrom are correct Britain's defence effort is in danger of being largely misdirected.

The balance of power in Europe, which since the beginning of the nineteenth century had been firmly based on France, then moved eastwards, so that at the start of the twentieth century it was concentrated with the so-called Central Powers, Germany and the Austro-Hungarian Empire. Despite defeat in 1918, economic and military power remained concentrated on the centre of Germany. In 1945 this changed. Germany, now divided, was occupied by a non-European power, the United States, two Western European states, Britain and France, and the Soviet Union.

The Western Allies disarmed rapidly, but the Red Army remained. The European balance of power had shifted eastwards once more, and now Britain, whose traditional policy of making alliances to preserve the balance of power in Europe, was faced with a new

European power, whose size and strength posed a potential military threat never before experienced by British policy-makers.

The nature of this threat was such that, for the first time, the United States with its traditional isolationist instincts, made firm military commitments to place, in peace-time, significant ground and air forces in Europe.

Britain did the same. It is an interesting paradox that although one of the long term aims of the Soviet Union had been to divide America and Europe, it was her presence in such overwhelming force in Central and Eastern Europe which linked them together so firmly after 1945. What then is the nature of this threat or is, as is sometimes claimed, the Soviet menace merely a mirror image of that posed by the United States and NATO? Do the Soviets indeed intend to wage war against Western Europe?

THE RISE OF RUSSIA AND HER EMPIRE

Russia's own history has been one of aggression. Aggression against herself. Starting in the twelfth and thirteenth centuries as a relatively small nation around Moscow, the Russians found themselves beset by enemies. The Golden Horde had swept in from the east and pressures had been felt from west and north. With no natural barriers the Russian nation began to substitute this deficiency with space. In this context there is a case for maintaining that Russian expansion was defensive in nature. Strong rulers were needed for such a people; thus, not only did the Russian nation grow with powerful autocratic leaders, but the people themselves at all levels developed xenophobic characteristics.

Recent experience, historically speaking, will have confirmed Russian suspicions, for they have been invaded three times from the west within the last two centuries, once by France and twice by Germany. The Soviet Union's drive westwards and subsequent setting up of a barrier of satellite, or at the very least small non-threatening neutral, countries on her western borders could therefore be construed as a defensive expansion, which was hopelessly misconstrued by the Western Allies. However, the advent of Lenin and the Russian Revolution substituted for an autocratic regime which was essentially defensively minded, an infinitely more ruthless autocratic regime, armed with a political creed which itself bore the seeds of a missionary driving force. For some twenty years, this new Revolutionary Government spent its time consolidating its grip on Russian society. It is said that some 5–10 million peasants were starved to death in order that the countryside should be brought into line with this new, industrially based, political philosophy.

The so-called patriotic war enabled Soviet Russia, aided by the United States and Britain, to defeat her main European enemy, Germany. She emerged from this war with a considerable industrial base, a vast army and, as subsequent events have shown, a network of spies and traitors prepared, on ideological grounds, to work for her. Just how much the intellectual community of the 1930s in the Western Democracies contributed, in real terms, to the scientific advances made by Communist Russia since 1941 may never be known. What is certain is that without the help of this small section of Western society, the Soviet Union's technological progress would have been far slower.

All this is good debating stuff but does it say anything about Soviet Russia's capabilities or intentions? More important, can the case for the USSR being the main threat against the West in general and Britain in particular be justified? Intentions can change. The perceived intentions of a potential adversary may be misconstrued. To rely on what a potential enemy may say as being a realistic guide to his intentions may be unwise. Capability, however, is a fact. Military capabilities can be measured, thus an enemy's capability is a more realistic basis upon which to plan, rather than upon any supposed intentions that he may or may not have. It is also possible, by examining a changing pattern of capability, to thereby deduce intentions. The USSR's essentially aggressive intentions can be deduced, not only by the basically Messianic Communist credo by which some of her leaders are motivated, not only by the traditional Russian desire to extend influence west and south, but by the pattern of Soviet Russia's military capabilities.

The historical Russian desire for 'warm water access' has been well documented in the past. The Eastern Question of the late nineteenth century was, in part, generated by the all pervading pressure exerted by the Tsars to dominate the Balkans and subsequently take over from the crumbling Ottoman Empire. Indeed, the Crimean War was fought not only to prop up the then corrupt regime in Turkey but to keep Russia out. Russia's historical drive for influence in SE Europe has never died and the discovery of oil in Persia (now Iran), Iraq and the Gulf has added strong strategic reasons for the present Soviet leadership to control this area of such strategic importance.

THE CHANGING NATURE OF THE SOVIET THREAT

There is one major area in which Soviet Russia's military capability has improved. This improvement has been so marked it has resulted, not just in a quantitative and qualitative improvement in a particular area of military capability, but in an additional capacity for projecting military power. This demonstrates unmistakably an intention towards the achievement of an actual military, economic and political domination worldwide.

In 1945 the USSR was a land power. Her naval forces were essentially defensive and their task in the West was to protect the extreme flanks of her land forces. Her air force had two roles – air defence and tactical support of the ground forces. This then was the actual perceived threat which faced Western Europe, in military terms, at the end of the Second World War. At this time, the USSR was not a nuclear power. Nevertheless this formidable military presence ensured that Communist Governments were installed in all the Central and Eastern European countries behind what became known as the Iron Curtain. The sheer size of the Red Army, combined with the exhaustion of Western Europe, did present an enormous foreign policy and military problem for each individual Western country. It became obvious at that time, and it is still true today, that no country, however large, could defend itself without allies. The North Atlantic Treaty Organisation (NATO) was created in 1949. For the first time in peace-time Western sovereign countries placed significant portions of their armed forces under the operational command or control of foreign officers. For the first time, the United States committed her forces to mainland Europe in peace-time. For the first time too, Britain had made a definitive commitment to keep four divisions in Germany.

The Soviet threat was against Continental Europe, thus for Britain to perceive her as the main threat was a logical extension of her traditional 'balance of power' foreign policy. One of the lessons of history is that if a power wishes to dominate Europe it will never succeed unless it can also dominate Britain. Hence if the Soviets do have it in mind ultimately to dominate Western Europe, they will clearly have to include Britain in their plans. Equally if Western Europe is to remain free, those countries forming NATO must stick together and, as far as the European countries are concerned, ensure that the United States remains a firm member of the Alliance.

What then of the threat? Originally this was essentially land based.

The Soviet Union and Warsaw Pact land forces have an overwhelming superiority in numbers. Although in 1941–5 the Red Army may have been relatively unsophisticated, it was immensely powerful in tanks. The great tank battles of the Second World War were not fought in the Western Desert, nor in NW Europe but on the plains of Russia. Her artillery, although mainly horse-drawn, was considerable. Indeed, only the Red Army carried out attacks in support of the artillery plans rather than the other way about. Training and planning were stereotyped and it was upon this apparent weakness, particularly at the lower levels of command, that NATO planners seized upon as a sign that the better equipped, better trained and more mobile smaller ground forces could survive against larger inflexible formations.

The Red Army deployed something in the order of two hundred divisions. By 1972 its order of battle consisted of 51 Tank Divisions, 106 Rifle Divisions and 7 Airborne Divisions. These were not all deployed against NATO. Nevertheless, the probable numbers of Warsaw Pact divisions facing NATO in the northern half of Germany, where the British Army of the Rhine is stationed, is in the order of 50 divisions against 12–14 divisions. Over the next decade, from the late 1940s to the late 1950s, this threat and the response to it, in military planning terms, remained much the same. NATO and Britain planned on the basis of the American nuclear monopoly. The overwhelming size of the Warsaw Pact ground forces was matched in fact, not by more mobile, albeit smaller, land forces, but by the planned immediate nuclear response to any aggression in Europe. This policy went under the name of the 'tripwire strategy'. The role of NATO land forces was to act as the tripwire which would set off the air forces – US then subsequently UK – to launch the nuclear strikes at the enemy.

The 1957 White Paper was produced in the context of NATO nuclear superiority, however by the mid-1960s the USSR too had developed her own nuclear weapons. Her land forces by this time had ceased to be the large motorised and horse-drawn formations of the 1940s. Soviet tank and artillery technology had one common feature, the equipments produced were effective, cheap and simple to maintain. Rifle divisions were becoming motor rifle divisions and, because National Service was still being maintained, she was building up a formidable number of reservists with military training experience.

By the mid-1970s, NATO threat presentations had changed their tune when referring to the 'inflexibility' of Russian training methods and command at unit level. In both Classified, Restricted and Unclassified briefings, reference was now made by Intelligence Officers from about 1969 onwards that the Soviet leadership was aware of this apparent defect. At the British Joint Warfare Establishment, which, amongst its other duties, was responsible for running courses and symposia for NATO officers, emphasis was certainly being laid on the noticeable improvement in the command and control of major WP exercises during the early 1970s. Indeed, at one time lecturers had to be reminded not to show the WP in too good a light – 'They may be six foot tall but not twelve foot, please.'[3]

THE NON-NUCLEAR MILITARY THREAT

The T72 tank had now been introduced and the balance of tanks to infantry and artillery within Warsaw Pact tank divisions and motor rifle divisions made it clear to NATO military planners that any major military aggression by the Warsaw Pact against the NATO Central Region, that is Western Germany, would be in overwhelming force at the chosen points of contact, would be well led and that certainly the aim would be to achieve, and then exploit, initial break-through with massive follow-up formations within 36 hours of the initial contact.

Not only were these ground forces equipped with their own short range tactical nuclear weapons but chemical (gas) attacks had to be assumed by NATO as being certain. Warsaw Pact and Red Army training is based on attack, and not on defence. Chemical attack is a part of normal training. Tactical doctrine as practised by all units and formations assumes the offensive use of chemical agents. Every Red Army formation has its own organic chemical unit and the emphasis placed then, and now, on chemical warfare has made it quite clear to NATO military planners that the Soviet capability is based on offence rather than defence. This is in stark contrast to NATO forces in the Central Region, and is one which must be taken into account both at the military and political level.

This emphasis on attack has been observed on all major WP exercises as well as in articles in their military journals. According to WP doctrine, pressure will be maintained continuously against defending forces and will continue day and night. Great value is placed on night movement and attack. Formations in contact will be relieved by follow-up divisions. WP doctrine foresees significant break-throughs being obtained at three or four points over a front that will immediately be exploited by pushing through major tank formations. These will have their own supporting infantry mounted in tracked armoured personnel carriers (APCs) and artillery, also tracked. Incidentally, another area of weakness used to be that the bulk of WP artillery was towed, hence vulnerable to counter battery and air to ground attack. Over the past fifteen years this imbalance has been corrected and now much of the WP artillery is, like NATO's, tracked.

Today, the mid-1980s, this ground threat is still a major factor. It is in the Central Region of NATO where the largest peace-time concentrations of both land and air forces are deployed. The Soviet Russian land threat is enhanced by her possession of seven airborne divisions. Of these, any two can be dropped simultaneously. This poses a significant strategic threat to European NATO. The great advantage that airborne forces have for the aggressor is that, so long as there is an observable airlift capacity, whilst they are uncommitted, their existence poses enormous problems to the defending commanders. The consequence is that reserve forces, which could otherwise be committed forward, might well have to be held back against the possible contingency of airborne landings well to the rear of NATO's main forces. Yet these very reserves may be needed to prevent the early break-through which every Warsaw Pact commander would be seeking to achieve. These airborne divisions also pose a threat to the NATO Northern Region (Norway, Denmark and Western Germany, north of the Elbe) as well as to the Southern Region (Greece, Turkey, Italy). Turkey and, to a lesser extent, Greece are particularly vulnerable not only because of the distances involved but also because their armies are relatively less mobile than those of the Central Region.

How efficient are these WP land forces? The experience, or rather observed experience, of the operations in Afghanistan would suggest that, at unit level, the Soviets still have much to learn. However, the sort of operations in Afghanistan are not those for which the bulk of the Russian Army is trained.

It is interesting to note that the US Army had the same problem in Vietnam, where much of the fighting was done at platoon, company and battalion level. It is these sorts of operations where leadership at junior and middle officer rank is so important and it is at this level that the British army has always excelled. The opinion of senior NATO officers is that, although it should not be overstated, the level of training and combat capacity of the Russian and Warsaw Pact front line divisions facing the Central Region is of a high order. Their equipment is good and they are trained to move forward quickly. They can sustain operations 24 hours a day moving fresh formations through the leading divisions, thus maintaining pressure on the defending units. They have the capacity to initiate or respond to nuclear strikes. Major rivers and canals do not constitute barriers as, not only do individual Warsaw Pact tanks and APCs have a swimming capability, but each major formation is equipped with mobile bridging equipment. It is little wonder then that the land threat posed by the Soviet and Warsaw Pact armies is regarded, and has been so regarded, by NATO planners as the major threat to NATO. However, this threat is essentially the same in the 1980s as it was in the late 1940s. Its improvement has been in quality. Fundamentally it has not changed.

THE NUCLEAR THREAT

There has, however, been a change since the early days of NATO. The USSR has become a nuclear power. As a superpower in her own right it was inevitable that she would seek to join the nuclear club. This she has done and has moved, within the space of some 37 years, from a position of total inferiority, through tactical and strategic inferiority, to partial superiority to a position now where many believe that the USSR is in a position of overall nuclear superiority against the United States. This position of superiority, if superiority it is, is not of itself sufficient to enable the USSR to exercise direct influence on the USA. What it has done, however, is to enable Russia to exercise her own non-nuclear military power with a freedom denied her in her days of undoubted nuclear inferiority.

A comparison of US and Soviet nuclear delivery systems both land based and sea launched in the year 1982–3 is shown below.

	US	*USSR*[4]
Inter-continental ballistic missiles	1572	2327
Intermediate and medium range ballistic missiles	39	606
Short range ballistic missiles	144	1212
Nuclear capable strike aircraft	982	3075

It is this changing nature of the overall Soviet threat which has led to various alterations to the way in which NATO's deterrent strategy is planned. We shall return to this particular NATO response in a later chapter.

THE MARITIME THREAT

The change in Soviet military forces in the non-nuclear field is in what has been referred to as the 'Unnoticed Challenge', a title given to a special report by Robert J. Hanks.[5] At the end of the Second World War the Red Navy was an inshore, defensively minded fleet whose prime aim was the security of the extreme flanks of the Red Army. The USSR, as a land power, had the perceptions of a land power and projected herself westwards by means of her land and air forces.

There has been much debate as to when the USSR first began to think in global maritime terms. There are those who maintain that the Cuban Missile Crisis in 1962 was the start of Russia's drive to achieve the status of a major maritime power. Certainly she was taught a lesson which she has never forgotten. That is, given the right circumstances, a navy, correctly constituted, can enable a state to influence events, without the ultimate use of force in anger, to an extreme extent not possible with either land or air forces. The United States was able to impose a blockade round Cuba by deploying an observable naval capability which was quite obviously able to achieve the stated aim, by force if necessary. Thus in the event no force in anger was ever used. The Russians, it is quite clear, have determined that they will never again be put into that position themselves. It is equally clear that they also intend that their own capability of being able to exert similar pressure should become a reality.

However, Admiral Gorshkov had been appointed Admiral of the Fleet by Khrushchev in the late 1950s. It is likely therefore that the Soviet Union had already begun to develop her maritime strategy at that time. The Cuban débâcle merely confirmed to the Kremlin leadership that Gorshkov's views, which almost certainly he had already been propounding, were correct.

Sergei Gorshkov is by any standards a remarkable military figure. He is possibly the greatest practical military thinker to emerge since the end of the Second World War. He has held the appointment of Commander-in-Chief of the Soviet Navy without a break since 1956. He is also Deputy Minister of Defence as well as being a senior and influential member of the Communist Party. Within a British context he would have been the First Sea Lord since before Suez, a Minister of

State in both Conservative and Labour Governments, as well as an influential party member of the party in power, permanently.

A gifted maritime theorist, it is certain that, not only will he have drawn the lessons of the campaigns in the Atlantic and Pacific, but he will have studied the history of Britain's Imperial past and the significant role that the Royal Navy played in its development and maintenance. As a naval strategist he will have studied the works of that great US Navy prophet, Admiral Alfred T. Mahan. He has obviously developed his own strategic thinking from these lessons of the past, from looking at the trends in US and UK maritime strategic thinking, and equally importantly, by seeing how current technology can enhance the capabilities already inherent in a well balanced 'blue water' fleet.

Being a military man he will have seen the futility of failing to match political aims and military objectives with resources. Russia's foreign policy aims in the long term can be seen quite clearly in the rise of the Red Navy. Gorshkov has been able to carry the Kremlin leadership with him and managed to persuade the political arm that, before it is able to succeed in its aims, it must actually create the necessary power to achieve those aims. The very success that has attended Gorshkov's efforts has been underlined, not only by the changing pattern of the content of the Red Navy, as its role changed from defence to offence, but also by the abject failure of British politicians to learn from these same lessons of the past.

When he first took over, Gorshkov was faced with two tasks, one of which had to be completed before the other could come to fruition. His first problem was to produce a navy with a surface fleet strong enough to take on and beat the NATO anti-submarine forces. He had in particular to be able to protect the Russian missile-carrying submarines. However, the one area where NATO navies were supreme was in aircraft carriers. His answer was to produce surface ships that were armed to the teeth to deal with two threats – ship to ship and air to ship simultaneously. An example of the sort of performance that the Red Navy expected from any one ship can be seen in a comparison between the 'Kara' class guided missile destroyer and the British 'Sheffield' class, both of which entered service with their respective fleets in the 1970s. While the Kara class destroyer has eight surface to surface missile launchers, as well as a further eight surface to air missiles and four 76 mm guns plus four 30 mm gatlings for point defence, the RN Sheffield class started life with one twin Sea Dart surface-to-air launcher, which could double up to act in the surface to surface role.[6]

It is quite obvious that the Russians, never too proud to learn from others, had seen that if a fleet was to be able to exercise influence in peace it must be seen to be capable of taking on, successfully, any potential enemy. It was equally obvious that the era of the battleship was past and that the aircraft carrier, alone amongst surface ships, was the only type of ship capable of producing at one and the same time a strategic threat and overwhelming tactical superiority.

Guns limit a ship's tactical area of influence by their range, say 15–30 miles. Missiles (surface to surface) have extended this range. For example, the estimated range of the later versions of the Russian SS-N-12 missile is 250 nautical miles. Helicopters armed with homing torpedoes, depth charges or air to surface missiles can also extend the immediate tactical area of influence for a ship. However, only an aircraft carrier has the means of projecting its tactical weaponry thousands of miles. The US Navy's Tomcat has a range of 2000 miles.

In addition, aircraft carriers will themselves carry a whole panoply of defensive and offensive weaponry, from airborne and shipborne early warning radar, air defence aircraft, attack aircraft, point defence surface to air missiles and guns as well as the facilities to control a task force, with which it will certainly be deployed.

The Red Navy began to take the first steps towards its eventual goal of being a worldwide strategic fleet both on the surface, as well as underneath, by the launching in the mid-1960s of two helicopter aircraft carriers, *Moskva* and *Leningrad.* These were designated anti-submarine cruisers but, as subsequent events showed, were forerunners, enabling the Red Navy to gain experience in carrier operations, of further developments in the aircraft carrier field. In 1970 *Kiev*, a 32 000 ton ship was laid down and is now operational. Although still referred to as an anti-submarine cruiser her surface-to-surface fire-power was that of a battleship, in stark contrast to the weaponry of *Invincible*, which was completed four years *after Kiev* had made her first operational cruise. The comparison is interesting and somewhat alarming for Britain.

Kiev

Eight SS-N-12s in four twin mountings (surface to surface).

Eight SA-N-3/4s (surface to air).

Invincible

One twin launcher (SS-N-1) anti-submarine.

One twin Sea Dart launcher, surface to air.

The creation of a significant submarine fleet carrying surface to surface long range or intermediate range nuclear weapons does not, in itself, produce a maritime threat. It is a part of the overall nuclear deterrent strategic posture of the nation that has nuclear weapons. Submarines have the advantage that they are, as yet, relatively invulnerable. To that extent they are the guarantee that the other side never has a genuine 'first strike' capability. It may well be that the weapon best able to deal with a missile carrying submarine is another submarine (hunter killer) or a combination of maritime aircraft and surface ships. The threat, however, is strategic and part and parcel of the whole threat which includes land based inter-continental ballistic missiles, air carried bombs or missiles and in the future maybe, satellites equipped with nuclear weapons.

The significance of the Red Navy's move into the carrier business is the motive behind such a move and the military capabilities which inevitably flow from such a move. This development must be taken by Britain within two contexts – global and in a narrow sense NATO. The Red Navy, together with its merchant fleet, controlled from the Ministry of Defence in Moscow, has achieved for the USSR the capability of projecting power and influence throughout the world. This influence is already being felt, not only in the price cutting war assiduously carried out by Soviet merchant skippers, at the very considerable expense of Western merchant fleets, but also in the activities of the Soviet fishing fleets.

THE 'PEACE-TIME' THREAT

The Americans are well aware that many a Russian 'trawler' is in fact a highly sophisticated electronic intelligence collector. In this particular field Russian activity is entirely uninhibited. As with their land based electronic intelligence operations, considerably more effort is put into this area than by the West. A comparison of merchant shipping in 1975 suffices to underline the point; 517 US merchant ships as against 1700 Russian. As far as fishing is concerned, the Russians deploy in the order of 4000 ocean going vessels. Operating in task forces of up to 100 ships with accompanying factory ships of the most modern kind, they are found in all the oceans of the world. They represent an economic activity which threatens the existence of those other national fleets. These operate on commercial lines and could, conceivably, be put out of business. The Soviet fishing fleet is therefore an actively used economic weapon of considerable importance.

As well, the Soviets have over 200 oceanic research and survey ships and these are observed continuously at work in all parts of the world. These different fleets operate essentially to further Russia's goal of achieving a form of economic and commercial maritime domination. Free from sound financial constraints they can, and do, make attractive offers to Third World countries in need of economic short term aid.

There is no area in the world where control of the sea lanes is vitally important, where Russian activity is not regularly observed or where the USSR has not actually taken some measure of control. These are areas of sea either bounded on both sides by land (Straits of Malacca) or where an unusually large number of ships pass in a congruence of sea lanes (Cape of Good Hope). It is no coincidence that, within two months of Britain announcing its historic decision during the Wilson Government that it was to complete withdrawal of its major commitments 'East of Suez', for the first time, the world saw a sizeable Soviet task force entering the Indian Ocean via the Strait of Malacca. Led by a Sverdlov class cruiser this force of five ships proceeded to visit India, Pakistan, Sri Lanka, Iraq, Iran, Somalia and Aden. Admiral Gorshkov himself went to India to meet his task force and this event signalled the start of a permanent Soviet presence in the Indian Ocean as well as the beginning of a much closer relationship between India and the Soviet Union.

The Soviets have permanent bases, or at the very least a permanent presence, in East Africa, Aden, West Africa and Vietnam. These facilities are, it must be remembered, in addition to their own ports. Thus, there is not one ocean or sea that the Soviet Union does not now have a presence at sea supported by a shore base of some sort. The North Atlantic is an exception.

That NATO is threatened in strategic terms by this Russian naval build up of 'blue water' capability cannot seriously be in question. Unfortunately, however, NATO, as an alliance of fully independent sovereign states, is unable, of itself, to take a worldwide view. Only three or, since the advent of Spain, four countries within the Alliance who appear to be able to take a strategic view of this maritime threat. However, even within NATO's own arbitrary boundaries, the local threat should be better understood than it appears to be.

NATO's military leaders have been aware for some time of the growing seriousness of the Soviet maritime threat to European

NATO. The political intentions of the Soviets are unmistakable. In a paper published by the Adam Smith Institute in 1983 the comment was made:

> It appears that the Soviet military and political leadership has identified two flank areas of NATO that are noticeably less well protected than the Central Front of Europe:
>
> A Northwestern flank comprising the lightly defended area stretching from the north cape of Norway through Iceland to the United Kingdom itself.[7]

THE NATO RESPONSE

The NATO military command structure reflects to some degree its areas of perceived interest. Its peace-time military structure formalises not only the political commitment but allows serious international military planning, on an alliance basis, to be carried out in peace. Within this military structure there are three levels of military commands:

(1) Major NATO Commands (MNCs) whose commanders are:

(a) Supreme Allied Commander Atlantic (SACLANT). Headquarters: Norfolk, Virginia, USA. Area of responsibility: West and East Atlantic, North Sea including Greenland and Iceland.
(b) Commander-in-Chief Channel (CINCHAN). Headquarters; Northwood, UK. Area of responsibility; Western Approaches and Channel. This officer also holds a second NATO appointment at the next lower level in which capacity he is subordinate to SACLANT. He is also C-in-C Eastern Atlantic (CINCEASTLANT), with responsibility for the North Sea.
(c) Supreme Allied Commander Europe (SACEUR). Headquarters: Mons, Belgium. Area of responsibility; from North Norway, Western Germany, Turkey, Greece, the Mediterranean, Spain and Portugal, the UK, Belgium and Holland. Note: Since France left the peace-time military structure, although remaining a full member of the Alliance, its area of responsibility excludes French territory but active military liaison continues.

(2) Major Subordinate Commands (MSC). These are joint commands in that they involve more than one service and, in general, the services of two or more countries.

There are a large number of MSCs and, because of the different needs and tasks of the three MNCs, there is no standard command chart. However, an example of an MSC is the Commander-in-Chief Central Region (CINCENT), headquarters: Brunsum, Belgium. This officer, a German, is responsible for the defence of Western Germany from the Elbe to the Austrian border as well as the security of the rear areas. He commands both land and air headquarters all of which are designated as Principal Subordinate Commands (PSC).

These are usually single service commands but 'joint' in that the forces of more than one country are involved. The Central Region PSC commanders are:

Commander Northern Army Group (COMNORTHAG)
Commander Central Army Group (COMCENTAG)
Commander Allied Air Forces Europe (COMAAFCE)
Commander 2nd Allied Tactical Air Force (COMTWOATAF)
Commander 4th Allied Tactical Air Force (COMFOURATAF)

All these officers are 'two hatted' in that, not only do they hold NATO appointments in peace-time, they also have national appointments. For instance, COMNORTHAG a British general, is also Commander-in-Chief British Army of the Rhine (C-in-C BAOR).

Below these officers are major single service nationally commanded formations, which formally come under the operational command or control of their respective NATO commanders at a certain stage in the alert procedures.

NATO is a maritime alliance. Of its three MNCs, two are wholly maritime. But even the third, Allied Command Europe (ACE) is influenced by the sea. Of its three MSCs, two are dominated by the sea. The air element is a common denominator in all NATO regions and there is the all-pervading threat of the USSR air arm. This is land- and ship-based. The problem of the Soviet air threat, and the implications it has, will be discussed later.

As far as the UK is concerned the Soviet naval threat is significant. Since the exploitation of the North Sea a new dimension to that area's strategic importance has emerged. The nature of this maritime threat is a totally new phenomenon in historical terms. This specific threat has been largely ignored by NATO's political leadership and to a lesser extent by its military. Further, there has been an obsession with the Central Region, and this obsession, partly for political reasons, partly for single service reasons, has become positively dangerous not only for the UK but also for NATO.

The USSR leadership has learnt from history. It has changed within the last thirty years from having a narrow land based strategic concept to that of a worldwide traditional maritime power. Sergei Gorshkov has no doubts about the role of this new instrument of power, the Red Navy. 'All of the modern great powers are maritime states . . . maritime states, having great economic capabilities have widely used their naval forces in peacetime to put pressure on their enemies.' He also intends that the Red Navy will be able to beat its opponents in war, as the design of his creation shows.

4 The Theatre Threat to European NATO

THE OVERALL PROBLEM

The Russian threat to the West is global. Not only can it be seen in purely military terms but also as an economic-politico threat. Control of the oil sources at present supplying the industrial needs of the West in general, and NATO countries in particular, is a vital interest. There is an identifiable requirement, in strategic terms, for NATO to take an interest in, and, if necessary, respond to, events which, although taking place outside the formal NATO boundaries, may require a concerted political and, *in extremis*, even a military response. There is also a need for NATO, in its capacity as a grouping of developed industrial democratic nations, to ensure that its fishing fleets are neither worked nor priced out of business by a Government-dominated, directed and subsidised, Soviet fishing fleet.

The same goes for the Western merchant fleets and in particular the British merchant service. To this specific subject we shall return, but for the moment it is sufficient to make the point that, an alliance such as NATO, whose member nations depend to a great extent on shipborne imports and exports, must, at some point, decide upon the irreducible size of its members' merchant shipping. The UK in particular, all of whose exports have, with very minor exceptions, to go by sea, must maintain a strategically viable merchant fleet operating under the national flag.

However, the Soviet threat specifically facing Europe in military terms has, in concert with its global strategy, also changed. It is the nature of this particular threat, and the areas in which it is peculiarly menacing that need to be examined before considering what the UK's specific responses ought to be, in European and national terms, within the NATO context. European NATO is divided into three regions, each with its own geographical peculiarities and political complications.

THE NORTHERN REGION

This takes in Norway, Spitsbergen, the Norwegian Sea, Jan Mayen Island, Greenland, Iceland, the Faroes as well as Denmark, the North Sea, the Baltic Approaches, Bornholm Island and Jutland.

This whole area is dominated by the sea. Norway is surrounded to the north, west and south by sea. Denmark also has sea to her north and west as well as to the east. Norway, one of the only two NATO countries to have a land frontier with Russia, presents strategic military problems both from her own and Russia's standpoints. Her geographical shape, a long slim country with the bulk of her population in the south, presents her defence planners with a unique problem – how to defend her extreme north. This defensive problem is compounded because North Norway, by being able to dominate the sea in that area, poses a specific problem for Russian planners. The Russian North Sea fleet, based at Murmansk, if it is to deploy into the Atlantic, must do so under the observation and within range of Norwegian (and/or NATO) air power, deployed in North Norway. And in winter shipping has to operate within 200 miles of the Norwegian coast. North Norway is therefore a piece of real estate of great strategic significance.

Denmark too is important in that, if the Russian Baltic fleet is to 'break out' it must do so before actual hostilities, in which case its deployment could be a clear signal of intention. Denmark is also a stepping stone to south Norway and both these area have airfields which if they fell into Russian hands, would mean that the UK would be in range of most of the Soviet ground attack aircraft at present in service. Possibly even more significant is that, once these airfields were in Russian hands, a direct parachute assault onto these islands would be possible without the transport aircraft having to cross NATO air defences deployed in Western Germany.

To see how important Norway is to NATO, we only need to look back to the Second World War. Just as the occupation of Norway and Denmark by Hitler was a vital strategic requirement before the attack on Russia could be launched, so too control of Norway by Russia could be a prelude to the application of decisive pressure on Western Germany.

> The Russian experience in World War II also indicated the supreme importance of coordination between the Soviet Union's northern and Baltic based military forces. Weakness in this context nearly cost Russia the war and has now been corrected.[8]

The successful defence of both North Norway and, to a slightly lesser extent, Denmark depends upon the timely arrival of sufficient reinforcements.

As far as north Norway is concerned, all the external forces (those from other NATO countries) must arrive by sea and air. Once in position they must be able to fight effectively against a numerically powerful enemy. Control of the air and sea will be vital and this can only be done with amphibious forces supported by effective anti-submarine (ASW), surface to air (SA) units as well as air power deployed in such a manner that its response to any threat is immediate, in strength, and effective. Hence these reinforcement forces must have the means of observation, early warning and control, or they can be taken out, at will, by the Soviet maritime and land based air forces.

THE CENTRAL REGION

Geographically this extends from the Elbe in the north to the German–Austrian border in the south. Westwards it can be taken to include France, which is not in peace-time a fully integrated partner in the NATO military structure, and the UK, which provides reinforcement units, both army and air force, to supplement those already deployed on the European Continent.

It is here that the industrial heart of Europe is located, with Germany the most economically powerful European member of NATO as the linchpin of Western European economic strength. Unlike the Northern Region where the NATO members, Norway and Denmark, do have specifically Scandinavian loyalties and interests, there is a more or less common view of the world and Europe's place in it. Now, divested of their colonial empires, Belgium's and Holland's interests, economic and strategic, are bound up entirely with NATO and the EEC. Through these two organisations, there is a cohesive drive which ensures that it is unlikely that their vital interests will conflict with each other or with those of Western Germany. It is therefore this region which can be considered the supreme prize. Clearly a threat to this area not only has to be taken seriously but, all other things being equal, ought to be regarded as the top priority in any defence strategy.

THE SOUTHERN REGION

As with the Northern Region the sea is the dominant factor. Again there is a narrow strait, the Dardanelles, which is a strategic choke point containing the Soviet Black Sea Fleet. Three of the NATO countries in this area are surrounded on three sides by sea – Turkey (the Black Sea and the Mediterranean), Greece (Aegean and the Mediterranean), and Italy. Spain, the latest NATO member, and France dominate the north-west end of the Mediterranean.

Similarity with the Northern Region continues as again, unlike the Central Region, there is a lack of political cohesiveness between the NATO partners which has in the past and can, in the future, prove a strategic danger. Turkey's view of the threat, for instance, is rather different from that of Belgium. Turkey has an interest in Afghanistan and Pakistan, as well as what is going on in Syria, Lebanon, Iraq and Iran, as she feels that she could be directly threatened by an escalation of conflict in these areas to her east and south-east. Yet, as these are outside NATO, her fellow NATO members have a perspective which may not be all that helpful.

The conflicts of interest between Greece and Turkey, not only over Cyprus but also over oil in the Aegean, are a source of concern to NATO and, naturally, an area where the USSR might well try, in her own interests, to stir the pot.

The Southern coast of the Mediterranean is the official limit of NATO's boundary. Yet here are a number of countries who have a great part to play in the general stability, or instability, in the area. Morocco, Tunisia, Libya, Algeria and Egypt all have their own national interests and specific ties to some NATO countries. Libya in particular is a problem, not only in that she might be used as a forward base by the USSR to outflank NATO, but also because she could become involved with the United States in a confrontation on a bilateral basis whilst it might be in European NATO countries' interests for friendly relations to be developed. Again this area of possible conflict is one which Russia might not be slow to exploit.

This then, in very brief outline, is the European NATO against which the USSR military threat is being projected. Russia's view of military power is that it is a legitimate tool with which to exert influence. The mere proximity of powerful forces may well produce a psychological effect upon the 'target' states so that, when they are confronted with diplomatic pressures, an accommodation can be reached. Such concessions then become enshrined as precedents and the game continues. This use of military power is not new and has been the classic means by which maritime powers have exerted influence. Russia is now such a power. To quote Gorshkov, 'All modern great powers are maritime states . . . maritime states having great economic capabilities have widely used their naval forces in peace-time to put pressure on their enemies.'[9] For instance, over the years, Norway's normal methods of resolving disputes with Russia has been to proceed quietly, avoiding provocations. However, she has encountered increasing problems as the USSR has adopted a more brazen attitude as her own military build-up has become more and more overwhelming.

The Soviet build-up on the Kola Peninsula, until 1945 a part of Finland, cannot be interpreted in any defensive context. Together with the actual military build-up in terms of units, there has been and still is an enormous effort in developing an infrastructure to support not only the military but also a programme of industrialisation, transportation and communications links.

> This activity, in turn, should be viewed in combination with the ambitious new virgin lands programme, an attempt to raise agricultural yields by 50% as well as to consolidate small towns into larger cities and to speed industrialisation in the vast non-black earth zone stretching from the Arctic frontier southwards beyond Moscow and from the Baltic States westward to the Urals. The total picture is one of building a secure rear base for defence in depth *as well as for possible thrusts beyond the Northern and Baltic boundaries.* [author's italics][10]

Murmansk, the world's largest city north of the Arctic Circle, became one of the main strategic centres of the Second World War. It has retained that significance as a virtually ice-free port and the home of the Soviet Northern Fleet. Murmansk Oblast was enlarged after the Second World War and now incorporates the old Finnish town of Petsamo. It not only is a base for part of the Northern Fleet, but also has Soviet naval infantry units, and is an exercise area for maritime and amphibious units. It is now a base for one of the Soviet herring fleets as well as having in its area nickel, copper and uranium mines.

SOVIET AIMS

As one of the main aims of the Soviet Union is the 'de-coupling' of America from European NATO, and hereby the demise of that alliance, it would appear that one of the aims of military build-up in the Kola Peninsula is to produce the observable military capability to achieve this objective by military means. Once this is achieved, we can assume that, in line with past and current Soviet doctrine on the peace-time use of military power, pressures will then be exerted on the Norwegians for neutralisation or even incorporation into the Soviet sphere of influence.

The Northern Region

This objective can be attained by the creation of maritime power and it is significant that the increase of military forces in the Kola Peninsula is in naval, maritime air and naval infantry units. These are the very type of units best able, by the use of amphibious exercises, cruises and other such shows of strength over, if necessary, significant periods of time, to produce in the mind of the target country a feeling of insecurity.

Strong Soviet diplomatic pressure is constantly being applied against the northern flank countries over boundary questions. One particular example is the dispute of the demarcation lines in the Barents Sea. On the one hand Norway has maintained that the median line, equidistant from the countries' borders and islands, should be the dividing line; yet Russia, using as a factor the military significance of the area, is determined to make use of the so-called sector principle. If granted, this would place the boundary along a straight line between the Norwegian/Soviet frontier and the North Pole which would have the effect of placing the demarcation line much closer to the Norwegian coast. There are also disagreements over the Continental Shelf and the rights of sovereignty over this. The possibility of economic finds of oil in these regions make these areas of dispute even more important and potentially dangerous.

In the Baltic, similar boundary issues have been originated by the Soviet Union. She has refused to accept the median principle in the Baltic of Gotland. There have been incidents at sea in the Baltic involving Danish, Soviet and East German ships. Both East German and Russian fishing boats have been intercepted in Norwegian and Danish national waters and even in areas specifically designated as prohibited.[11]

These eavesdropping activities which of course perform two functions – the genuine gathering of military intelligence as well as the continuance of a climate of pressure – are by no means confined to the sea. The Northern Region countries are subjected to another means of information gathering:

> Heavy road transport vehicles filled with electronic equipment are being used by Warsaw Pact countries as a land equivalent to spy trawlers to collect intelligence information in Scandinavia. The spy vehicles travel regularly from the Soviet Union through Finland, Sweden and Denmark and then cross by ferry to East Germany. They carry the international TIR road haulage carnet which permits them to pass without being examined by customs officials when they cross national boundaries . . . They are able to stop for a day or two at a parking site to trace military communications in the area without exciting suspicion. It is also relatively simple for them to have a breakdown or a rest at a roadside near military installations.[12]

The Central Region

In the Central Region, Russia's peace-time uses of politico-military pressures are somewhat different. This reflects the different political and military situations in the Central Region. Here is gathered the greatest concentration of land and air power, in conventional terms, of both NATO and the Warsaw Pact. Because of this concentration of power it is possible to conceive that, in some ways, there is a greater military stability in the region.

Certainly, in political terms, as far as the West is concerned, there is much more cohesiveness of effort. All the Western European powers in the centre, and this includes France and Britain, are members both of NATO and the EEC. This is in contrast to the Northern Region where Norway, although a NATO country, is not in the EEC. Sweden is in neither, Finland has a peculiar relationship with Russia, whilst Denmark belongs both to NATO and the EEC. Portugal and Spain are not considered as Central Region powers in the context of this argument, as their political and geographical relationships with NATO and the EEC are, particularly in the case of Spain, more dynamic than those of the more industrial nations in the geographical centre of Continental Europe.

Sheer military pressures are less easy for Russia to apply to the Central Region than in either the Northern or Southern Regions of NATO. This is because maritime and naval power by its ability to conduct exercises, and cruises of task forces in international waters for long periods of time is in many ways a more suitable medium for the pressure of a 'visible presence' than are ground and land based air forces. There are after all no international land masses, excluding the possible exceptions of the polar regions, thus armies are restricted in their 'shows of strength' to the territories of their own countries or those of their allies.

In peace-time therefore the USSR has concentrated her efforts in destabilising the alliance in the Central Region by directing her efforts to the gathering of intelligence by the use of electronic intelligence (ELINT), spying and the influencing of opinion in Western Europe against the United States and, in particular, against the nuclear strategy of the alliance.

Despite the fact that NATO's greatest concentration of non-nuclear force is in the Central Region, there is still a considerable imbalance in favour of the Warsaw Pact. The significance of this upon NATO's defence strategy is marked. It is worthwhile making the point here that deterrence and defence are not quite the same thing. It is the failure of Western leaders to get this truth across which has enabled the Soviets, by blurring this truth, to cast considerable doubts upon the nuclear strategy of the West. It is in the Central Region where this campaign has been waged most successfully.

Before a defence strategy can prove itself, deterrence must have failed. However, in part, a defence strategy if it appears to be realistic can be an element, indeed an important part, of the overall strategic deterrent posture.

The Problem of Numbers

One of the problems facing NATO planners in the Central Region, for instance, is the overwhelming numbers of tanks at present deployed by the Warsaw Pact forces stationed in Eastern Europe and western Russia. Of course, the counter, in defensive terms, against tanks is not just tanks. Anti-tank weapons, hand held by the individual infantrymen, heavier anti-tank guns and rocket launchers, possibly manned by artillerymen, supported by air launched weapons from helicopters or fighter ground attack aircraft (FGA) will all contribute with the main battle tank to the overall defence against the Warsaw Pact armoured formations. Even so, the balance is heavily in favour of the aggressor, who can choose his points of contact ensuring that he can achieve a local superiority of, say, 7:1, far in excess of the traditional 3:1 normally required to produce tactical success.

One way of correcting this obvious military weakness would be to introduce a weapon capable of destroying large numbers of tanks advancing in concentrations. Nuclear weapons is an answer. Equally obvious, quite apart from the political inhibitions on the use of any nuclear weapons, is that the widespread damage not only to property, buildings, woods, etc. but to the civil population could well make these weapons unacceptable to the military commanders even after 'nuclear release'.

The invention of the enhanced radiation warhead, the neutron bomb, however, removed these disadvantages. Here, for the first time, was a nuclear warhead which, when burst, would produce relatively little blast effect but considerable radiation effect. With an accurate means of delivery, the neutron warhead would give to a ground commander the ability to destroy attacking armoured forces without the mass destruction normally associated with the use of tactical nuclear weapons. The Warsaw Pact campaign against the deployment of these weapons was brilliantly successful.

Peace movements sprang up and the most extraordinary arguments were produced to stop its deployment. Few of the arguments were based on military realities. Nevertheless, such a head of steam was raised that NATO's political leaders pulled back and the neutron weapon was not deployed, thus leaving the massive conventional military imbalance between the Central Region land forces a major problem for the military planners charged with developing the defensive strategy for the West in the event of deterrence failing. To the extent that this area of weakness must be quite obvious to the Soviet military and political leadership, this cannot but have a debilitating influence on NATO's overall deterrent posture.

This same technique has been used over the deployment of the Cruise and Pershing missiles and their launchers in Europe. In simple terms the USSR produced a new level of nuclear weaponry. The SS20, a land based intermediate range missile (INF) system with three warheads per missile, began to be deployed in the mid-1970s. This class of weapon was not matched by NATO and, in 1979, the European NATO countries, concerned that NATO's deterrence strategy would thereby begin to lose some of its credibility, 'decided on a dual track decision, in which NATO agreed to deploy US longer range INF missiles whilst simultaneously offering US–Soviet arms control negotiations on INF'.[13] Despite the fact that the Soviet Union produced no meaningful proposals and that the warning over the proposed deployment of Cruise missiles was given years ahead of the event, the so-called Peace Movements in Western Europe, got to work. Those in Germany, Holland and the UK campaigned hard on the basis that this deployment was an escalation of the nuclear arms race. However, no doubt having learnt from the neutron bomb episode, European NATO leaders stood firm. Their firmness was undoubtedly helped by the severe defeats that the unilateralists suffered in both the West German and British general elections held in 1983. The Central Region therefore is not one where Soviet military power is directly used to influence the political leadership but, as we have shown, much use in made of 'peace' movements.

The Southern Region

The Southern Region has more similarities with the Northern Region than it does with the Central Region. Here the sea dominates. There is the combination of Soviet naval power and the injection of military equipment and advisers in the Arab/Israel confrontation, specifically in the Lebanon to consider. It is no part of this book to postulate possible scenarios to the Arab/Israeli confrontation. However, it is in this area that Turkey's vital interests are at stake. It is interesting to see how at NATO briefings the perception of 'the threat' is significantly different from that presented by Turkish officers wearing their national hats or when they spoke as CENTO (Central Treaty Organisation) officers. It is also in this area that United States national interests may well be perceived to be at stake, whilst the European NATO countries might easily prefer different approaches to the whole problem. Here, therefore, is an area where a conflict of interest between NATO countries might take place.

From the NATO military planners' viewpoint, the danger of a *de facto* outflanking of NATO forces in this region by the USSR using, say, Libya is a factor which must be taken into account. However, the NATO naval presence is significant and NATO's own perception of the importance of the sea to the defence of this region is shown by the fact that the overall commander, a NATO Major Subordinate Command (MSC), is an American admiral and his most powerful Principal Subordinate Commander (PSC), Commander Strike Force South, (COMSTIKFORSOUTH) is also a US navy officer. In fact he is, in peace-time, the Commander US 6th Fleet, and as such not only has powerful naval forces under his command but also the most powerful, in terms of strike power, air force, being the carrier based naval aviation units.

That the Soviets have long regarded the US 6th Fleet as the key to the military defence of the Southern Region is fairly obvious. Until the rate of incidents grew too much, and too dangerous, for even the Red Navy, the 6th Fleet, and RN task forces when deployed, were constantly harassed by Soviet ships. Indeed 'in 1973 it was all in the day's work for groups of Soviet ships to make dummy attacks on the carriers of the 6th Fleet'.[14] Both the Soviet and US navies in the Mediterranean are constantly at a high state of alert. One cannot speak for the Soviet Navy but certainly every Soviet submarine discovered in the Mediterranean is thereafter 'marked'. This means that the submarine is kept under surveillance and weapons are aimed at it so that, at a moment's notice, it can be attacked.

SOVIET OPTIONS

The aim of this chapter has been to show that the Soviet Union will do its utmost, whilst at the same time avoiding a direct military confrontation, particularly with the United States, to undermine the cohesion of NATO's European Northern Region. As the base for its Northern Fleet can be overlooked from military installations in north Norway, Soviet naval power will be used in peace-time to produce a feeling of isolation in the minds of the local Norwegian population and military commanders. Any military operations involving the deployment of the Northern Fleet for war would certainly be preceded by the attempted military occupation of north Norway, if that country has not previously been separated politically, or at least militarily, from the rest of NATO. Surprise attack is a real option in this area and, as there is no strategic depth in the NATO defences, the possibility of Norway being cut off by the Russian North Fleet is very real. Much the same goes for the Baltic. It is worth remembering that the Russians do not think in terms of 'flanks' but in 'theatres of military operations'. That the security of this 'TVD' is a vital precondition to the military defeat of the NATO Central Region should not be forgotten.

In the Central Region the sheer magnitude of the military power on both sides is a form of security. Russian doctrine requires that success is certain before operations are mounted. And, although little preparatory deployment is needed by the Warsaw Pact, an attack in this region is almost certainly going to lead to nuclear war in contrast, possibly, to military adventures elsewhere.

In the Southern Region political means to achieve a balance of power decisively unfavourable to NATO are quite possible. Again the political tensions between NATO countries themselves are quite sufficient to give NATO ministers sleepless nights even without Russian interference.

SOVIET MILITARY DOCTRINE

Before considering NATO's own response in the event of hostilities, it is worth looking at Soviet military doctrine so as to see the sort of operations that might be mounted against European NATO. If such operations are mounted, deterrence has failed. Even so it may well be that nuclear weapons will not be used. This is just as well for, although one can imagine what kind of conventional operations might take place and design a number of scenarios, no one can really tell what will happen after nuclear weapons have been used.

> In the Northern Region Soviet doctrine postulates a short, very intense war creating a territorial *fait accompli* before the Nordic countries have the opportunity to mobilise or even to take the political steps necessary to place their forces under NATO. Such operations will be undertaken by simultaneous attacks across the land frontier, attacks across neutral Sweden and probably Finland with the aim of cutting Norway in half. Quite possibly parachute forces will be dropped onto Norwegian (potentially NATO) installations such as airfields. Amphibious landings will be made to support all these attacks whilst at the same time the Northern Fleet will have deployed a submarine screen to contest the possible approach of NATO reinforcements. Landings could also be made on the Lofoten Islands, Bear Island and even Iceland and Jan Mayen Island.[15]

Soviet writings stress the interdependency of sea supremacy and ground and air combat operations within a military theatre. Of particular relevance to the success of any operations against Norway are those of Hitler's Germany in 1940 where strategic, as well as tactical, surprise was achieved. It may also be worth remembering that one of the factors which must have had an effect on Britain's lack of preparedness for the 1940 invasion of Norway was that her eyes were firmly fixed on the, then, Western front. If the Soviets ever established themselves in North Norway they could not be ejected by conventional military forces within the foreseeable future. Speed and surprise, therefore, will be their main aim.

The problems posed in the Central Region for Soviet planners are somewhat different. Quite apart from the reliability, or otherwise, which they can put on their own Eastern European allies to join in any major aggression against the West, the physical presence, in considerable strength, of the Americans makes it unlikely that any sizeable military advances could be made without involving US forces, and almost certainly US casualties. However, this is a possibility that has to be considered. On the basis that the Soviets would not actually attempt a military assault against Western Germany unless certain of a quick tactical victory which they could then present to NATO as a negotiating position, we must assume that any such attack would be sudden and in considerable strength. Without, at this stage, going into numbers, how might the Warsaw Pact attack?

First of all, organisation and training; the basic fighting formation in the Soviet Army is the division. Below this level training and command responsibility is considerably more rigid than in the British Army. Essentially two types of division will oppose NATO forces in the Central Region – the tank division and mortar rifle division. Both combine tank, infantry and artillery units although, as their names imply, the proportion of tank units to infantry units is different. These divisions will also be further supported by artillery formations allotted by higher headquarters.

Russian doctrine sees mobility and continuous pressure being essential elements of attack. Thus any advance will be initially across a wide front. However anticipated thrust lines will have been selected on the basis of geography and the known dispositions of the defending forces. Leading divisions will be ruthlessly used and, as they become ineffective due to casualties, follow-up divisions will 'fight through them'. Thus defending formations will be under constant pressure. Once breakthroughs have been achieved these will be immediately exploited by the passing through of tank formations. These operations will continue 24 hours a day and will be supported by tactical ground attack aircraft, a highly effective wireless and electronic jamming organisation whose function will be to disrupt, if not stop, defending HQs communications systems. One of the most ominous factors which must be a constant source of worry to all NATO and national planners is the fact that all WP formations train on the basis that the use of chemical agents is assumed.

THE CHEMICAL THREAT[16]

Every Russian unit of battalion strength and over has its own chemical sub-unit or unit. Chemical weapons are regarded, it appears, in the same light as artillery – a means of neutralising a defence so that exploitation can be carried out by the advancing tank and infantry formations. The effects on a defence of chemical attacks are hard to envisage. However, it is clear that, even with plenty of warning so that a unit can take the necessary precautions, its efficiency will be reduced. The state that an individual soldier will be in after strenuous and stressful activity for a number of hours whilst dressed in his protective clothing (referred to as the 'Noddy' suit) will be pretty bad. Even the threat of chemical attacks may lead units to dress themselves in their 'Noddy' suits. That these soldiers could be faced with continuous fighting against attacking units which themselves may be being replaced by fresh formations is a daunting prospect.

THE CONVENTIONAL TACTICAL POSSIBILITIES

At the main points of contact where the Warsaw Pact army and front commanders hope to achieve break-through, they would aim to achieve a local superiority of something in the order of 7:1. The discovery of the whereabouts of NATO reserve formations would be near the top of the list of priorities for the supporting tactical air forces and, once found, they would immediately be attacked. Certainly movement by day of reserves would be dangerous and Warsaw Pact commanders would plan to ensure that, as far as possible, NATO commanders would be unable, at least in daylight, to start plugging the gaps. Speed and momentum will assist in maintaining any local tactical advantage.

Whether any attack against the Central Region could have a limited objective – that is, an objective which falls short of an overwhelming victory against all the ground and air forces in Western Germany – is difficult to imagine. One could postulate a rapid attack north of the Elbe to take out Jutland and Denmark, and possibly Hamburg, within 24 hours, followed by a much publicised offer to negotiate. One could imagine an attack against, say, the Northern Army Group to produce a *de facto* situation from which negotiations can proceed. The point about these two possibilities is that it is just conceivable that US land forces might not be involved. However, whether limited or not, any aggression against the Central Region would have to be in strength, would involve the move of 2nd echelon forces from Western Russia and would certainly be met by the combined air forces of NATO commanded by, and of course including, US personnel.

For this reason therefore, although an interesting exercise in scenario production, it is probable that the one area in European NATO where an attack with limited politico-military objectives is most unlikely to take place is the Central Region.

The Southern Region has some similarities with the Northern Region. Essentially this is a naval theatre. Because of the present political scene in the area being so fraught, it is not worth even to try to postulate a limited war, or the beginnings of a general war situation in this region. However, clearly the prime objective of any Soviet war plans for this area will be the elimination of the US 6th Fleet as, if this was achieved, the whole military balance in the Region, even before the start of land/air operations, would be completely upset. Turkey would be isolated. Greece and Italy one suspects would not be considered in the initial stages of vital strategic importance without the support of the 6th Fleet, as their geographical locations are not so relevant to the strategic security of the Central Region as those of Norway and Denmark.

Against this formidable threat to Western Europe, NATO has formulated its own plans. Great Britain, as a NATO partner, has helped in the development of these plans. However, every country has its own interests, both political and strategic, to consider. Ideally NATO's interests and national interests coincide. If they do not then hard decisions may have to be taken. The time has now come when these decisions, in the interests of both NATO and the UK, must be taken.

5 The Problems of Conventional Defence in Europe

The main problem facing NATO is the fact that for over thirty years it has only appeared to consider a conventional war in Europe of being in the Central Front and of short duration. This single scenario syndrome, which admittedly does postulate the two extreme possibilities, an attack with little or no warning or an attack after a WP build-up of, say, three to four weeks, characterises the obsession that the European Command has had, and still has, with the Central Front.

Despite the formidable rise of the Soviet Navy and the strength and nature of the Northern Fleet in particular, NATO planners and generations of UK Defence Ministers give the appearance of continuing to plan as if the Soviet Navy did not exist. This is of course an over-statement but, to illustrate the point, on 16 May 1983 a report on 'Strengthening Conventional Deterrence in Europe' was published.[17]

The Steering Group members under whose advice the report was compiled, were all distinguished service officers and academics (including six officers of General or equivalent rank, thirteen professors and three senior politicians). This report, which makes excellent reading, has not one word about naval operations. Neither Norway nor Denmark are mentioned. It is clear that the thought that the Soviets might conduct naval operations only against European NATO has not even been considered. If the lessons of 1940 still have some validity, then it would seem that the Soviets might well consider that, if the stage was ever reached in which they should engage in military operations against NATO, the area in which to conduct such operations might well be in the NATO Northern Region. NATO forces in this region are not strong and rely heavily on reinforcements. US Forces in Europe would not immediately be involved, which, assuming a limited political and military aim, could suit the Soviets.

Furthermore the Central European WP powers would not be involved, thus keeping in the background a major imponderable for Moscow planners, the reliability of the East European WP members.

The possibility of a major Soviet incursion into North Norway with simultaneous landings in Spitzbergen, Bear Island, Jan Mayen Island and possibly Iceland, to support the passage of the Northern Fleet into the Eastern Atlantic is one which NATO planners may have faced. It seems certain that UK politicians have not. The 1981 White Paper demonstrated that Whitehall's eyes were firmly fixed on the Central Front and the 1983 White Paper, whilst genuflecting towards 'the lesson of the Falklands', goes the same way. There is a very powerful Central Front lobby in NATO and London. Its influence is now at the stage of being positively dangerous both to the security of the UK and to NATO.

STRATEGIC CONCEPTS AND NUMBERS

In the early days of the alliance the military contribution by the Europeans was to provide sufficient conventional ground and air forces in order to produce the necessary 'tripwire' which, if aggression had taken place, would set off the American Nuclear Strategic Forces against the WP and Soviet Union. However, this simple doctrine was put to the test psychologically at the time of the Korean War (1951–3).

> When the Korean War first raised the spectre of a Soviet attack on Europe, NATO developed the Lisbon goals, which envisaged a largely conventional defence of Europe. These provided for some thirty-five to forty regular and some fifty-five to sixty reserve divisions. It soon became apparent, however, that no European ally was prepared to make the sacrifices necessary to raise these forces.[18]

It is clear that no European ally has ever been remotely prepared to meet these goals then or since. Yet today we have a Strategy of Flexible Response which, by its very nature, needs strong conventional land forces in the Central Region in particular. Combine this with, particularly in the Central Region, a forward defence posture, and the requirement is for even stronger conventional forces. These are simply not forthcoming. Nor will they be. One has to say that in the field of defence, politicians all too frequently produce political requirements without really going into the military consequences of those requirements. It must also be said that some Defence Ministers have known perfectly well what the military requirements are for a particular task, but have either deliberately fudged the issue or ignored it. Any defence policy based on a fraud will, in the end, fail for one of two reasons. Either it will become incredible to the servicemen charged with carrying it out, with a consequent rise of disillusionment and fall in morale, and this can spill over into the general civilian population. This may, in time, result in a widespread 'lack of will'. It might also become incredible to the potential aggressor. This, at worst, may cast doubts in the aggressor's mind about the reality of other aspects of other national and NATO defence postures, the nuclear based deterrence for instance. In this respect it is vital for NATO to have, and be seen to have, realistic levels of conventional forces of the right kind, in the right place. It is only then that such forces can underpin the nuclear deterrent strategy.

The arrival of the Eisenhower presidency resulted in a new look for the defence in Europe. The USA introduced the Radford Plan. This started with the assumption that NATO forces would always be inferior to the vast conscript Soviet forces. A non-nuclear conventional defence was not on. The logical next step, once a nuclear based defence was assumed, was to introduce tactical nuclear weapons based in Europe. Many of these were short range ground launched FFRs (Corporal, Honest John, Sergeant, and, at present, Lance). These were operated under a 'double veto' system; what we now refer to as the 'dual key'. 'However, some of these systems were of a range and yield that made them indistinguishable from those in the arsenal of the Strategic Air Command (SAC).'[19]

They were tactical weapons only in the sense that they were deployed under the operational command of SACEUR and not the Strategic Air Command (SAC) commander. The question of what is tactical and what is strategic was relatively simple in the 1950s when, because of the NATO (US) nuclear superiority, the Soviet views on this matter were not too important. Today, the situation is somewhat different and what the Soviets think about these matters is vital. Indeed, a paradox facing both NATO and WP is the need for a large measure of agreement on the nuclear ground rules. A return, almost, to the Middle Ages, when wars were fought within well known conventions which were, on the whole, kept to. Whether or not deterrence can be maintained whilst at the same time both sides observe certain restrictions is one of the major questions of this and the next centuries. Certainly the fact that a major strategic confrontation, which is more or less permanent, can take place, whilst at the same time various arms limitation talks and signed agreements, can also proceed, leads one to the hope that there is indeed the possibility of agreed parameters within which both sides will operate. Mutual confidence can be the outcome of strength, but this strength must be balanced and it must be realistic at all levels of combat capability, both conventional and nuclear.

THE IMPLICATIONS OF FLEXIBLE RESPONSE

The moves in NATO towards the notion that there is a possibility of a period of non-nuclear war between itself and the WP places considerable strains upon the alliance. The motives behind such a strategy must be examined extremely carefully, for the development of the flexible (forward defence) response strategy has been a shift of emphasis in strategic thought and practice far greater than people have realised. The political reasons for the introduction of the forward defence strategy in the Central Region are obvious enough. If NATO forces pulled back as little as 100 miles on the Central Front, the Federal Republic of Germany would have lost the greater part of its territory. What might have been tolerable for the alliance in strategic terms could well be intolerable for a single state. NATO is an alliance of sovereign states, and no individual state within that alliance will support a strategy, the outcome of which would result in the loss of its own sovereignty.

It is interesting that, until the mid-1960s, the European NATO countries felt that an immediate nuclear response strategy was in their best interests. Talk of strengthening conventional capabilities was regarded with suspicion, as the fear in European capitals was that there could be a lessening of United States resolve. What the Europeans wanted was an absolute commitment to their defence and one way of going a long way to ensure this was a weak, in conventional terms, European NATO, which meant that security could not possibly be found in a defensive capability, but only in deterrence. This desire for reassurance was described by Kissinger when he said:

> Washington has at times shown signs of impatience towards the German leaders and their frequent need for reassurance. Secretary Rusk has been reported more than once to be restless with what he has called the 'pledging sessions' which the Germans seem so often to demand.[20]

Now that the flexible response is with us, it may be worth considering why, as this could affect the strategic decisions in the level of conventional forces. The problem here is credibility; that is the credibility of the American nuclear deterrent. In the mid-1960s, the gestation period of the flexible response, the US Defence Secretary, McNamara, believed that a build-up of European NATO's conventional forces would enhance the overall nuclear deterrent strategy. He stated:

> if we have shown ourselves able and ready to engage in large scale non-nuclear warfare in response to a Communist provocation, the Soviets can hardly misconstrue two things: first, that we regard this provocation as a challenge to our vital interests; and second, that we will use nuclear weapons to prevail, if this became necessary.[21]

As a technical assessment this may have had merit. However, it was at the time unconvincing to the European NATO powers. Flexible response was great when applied to, say, South America or the Middle East, but when referred to the Central Region then, to the Europeans, it made less sense.

Flexible response in the Central Region makes sense if the Soviets conducted limited operations with limited aims. But is a limited attack in the Central Region, of all the NATO command areas, a realistic scenario? Intentions are difficult to assess, it is capabilities that count. How does NATO decide that an aggression is limited? Any attack in the early stages is bound to be limited in the sense that initial success is going to be limited in the amount of NATO territory taken. When and how will NATO commanders decide that the aggression is more than limited, and in any case who defines limited? An attack can be limited to taking out Hamburg, West Germany north of the Elbe, and Denmark, or it could be limited to the Northern Army Group area of responsibility. In such situations, Denmark's perception and West Germany's views will certainly be different from those of France, the United States and Spain, even if the Soviets had made public their self-imposed limitations. This essential weakness in the flexible response strategy, itelf born from the lessening of the nuclear deterrent credibility of the US in the face of Russia's own growing nuclear strength in both strategic and tactical nuclear arms, was apparent to the Germans. The forward defence posture is consequent to the political requirement to present the flexible response in a more acceptable form to the German people. However, does it make military sense? If it does not at present, what needs to be done in the military field to maintain the credibility of the military plans? Here again we are faced with political decisions being taken and the inevitable military consequences being ignored or fudged. The point is that, if the forward defence strategy is not going to work because of lack of resources, we are in danger of a *de facto* return to the immediate nuclear response strategy.

This problem has not suddenly come upon NATO. It was inherent when the Americans first began to argue for an increase in the strength of NATO's conventional forces. At the beginning, it used to be said, the purpose of the conventional forces was to provide a pause in military operations to permit the Soviets to consider the risks involved in continuing. On NATO's side, the consequent loss of ground was presumably to be regarded as 'flexibility'. All that this strategic fudging was achieving was an attempt to paper over somehow the growing incredibility in European minds, let alone the Soviets, of the firmness of the American nuclear deterrent in the face of the growing WP threat.

One has to ask the question: if the Soviets ever did engage in military operations in the Central Region, would they not have carefully considered the NATO nuclear response? Presumably, in the case postulated, they would have discounted it. Why should anyone imagine that at the end of a pause, NATO will still be in as good a tactical position as she was at the beginning of hostilities? What if at that time the Soviet Union offered to negotiate, with, say, a large tract of West German territory with a few medium size towns in WP hands? Henry Kissinger posed the one question which has never really been answered:

> If nuclear war is too risky for the West at the start of the conflict, why should it not be even more risky when the local issue has in effect already been decided and when the devastation caused by a nuclear exchange may make the local situation seem irrelevant? If on the other hand, it is argued that the Soviets would never dare to defeat NATO's ground forces lest this trigger a nuclear exchange, what is gained by increasing the number of NATO divisions beyond a level which forces the Soviets into a major commitment?[22]

It is of interest that Kissinger was thinking, by reference to ground forces, of operations on land (the Central Front?). Was this not another example of the possibility of sea–air operations taking place not being considered at the political level?

Defence and deterrence are not the same. Nuclear deterrence is in a sense a relatively simple concept. It is based on the certainty that no one can win a nuclear war and, unless the aggressor is able to inflict virtual annihilation on the other side's nuclear forces (the first strike capability), then he will, in turn, be devastated by the nuclear response. An observable second strike capability is surely the ultimate deterrent between nuclear superpowers. There is now a grey area of deterrence because the nuclear superpowers may be prepared to see a lower level of military force used before being forced to consider the use of the ultimate weapon. Herein lies the problem. How far can one read the mind of one's opponent? It is arguable that both the Kaiser and Hitler were surprised at Great Britain's reaction in 1914 and 1939. Certainly the Foreign Office had totally misread the Argentine intentions in 1982. The Israelis, of all people, got it wrong at the start of the Egyptian campaign on the Day of Atonement.

In the military equation, it is capabilities that count, not intentions. Intentions can change over night; capabilities are facts and, once lost, are almost impossible to regain. All too often British governments, both Conservative and Labour, have allowed certain strategic and tactical capabilities to fall away whilst the defence commitments, for which those same capabilities were necessary, remained. In this respect, one has to say that Conservative Defence Ministers have a far worse record than their Labour opposite numbers. It is an interesting paradox that, whereas the Conservative Parliamentary Party has the right instincts for defence, their Front Bench have constantly made a nonsense of defence policy, whereas the opposite has often applied in the case of the Labour Party.

So, with so-called conventional deterrence, NATO is immediately faced with the uncertainties inherent in any non-nuclear posture. What is the deterrent value of a division? At what level does air power need to be deployed before it becomes a deterrent rather than one of the factors in the military appreciation. (Appreciations are the process by which military planners assemble all the facts – factors – then look at the options – courses open – both to the enemy and to the friendly forces before finally coming up with recommended solution together with alternatives. At that point, the political and command decisions are taken and the 'plans' produced.)

The deterrent value of conventional forces might lie in overwhelming numbers. Yet even this is not enough. In 1914, Germany was not deterred by numbers but, indeed, decided in part to go to war before the Russians could complete their mobilisation. Fear of numbers in this case having the opposite effect. Numbers of 'in place' formations may be more relevant. In this respect 'mal-deployment' of large numbers of NATO forces in peace-time is still with us after nearly thirty-five years. The possibility of a surprise attack producing sufficient success quickly, so that a negotiating position is established, cannot be ruled out as far as conventional operations are concerned.

However, these strategies are with us. For political reasons, immediate nuclear response may not be a feasible doctrine, despite the fact that, in the past, it has been effective (at least we know that it was not ineffective). Yet the very fact that there is so much debate on NATO's current strategy shows that, as yet, no equally credible strategic posture has replaced it. A strategic doctrine is of no use if it is not buttressed with the necessary elements of political will and military power.

THE PROBLEMS OF FORWARD DEFENCE

Let us consider then the military implications in each European NATO region of the forward defence posture as a part of the overall flexible response. As the greatest land/air confrontation in peace-time is the Central Region and it is the pressures of that region that seem to bear most heavily on NATO ministers and planners, let us consider this first.

The first and most obvious factor is the disparity of numbers. Despite the so-called Lisbon goals, none of the European powers in the Central Region have gone anywhere near even making an attempt to produce the number of regular, let alone reserve divisions, to produce a realistic non-nuclear defensive posture. By making the most optimistic forecasts, it is possible to postulate that a WP land/air attack on the Central Region could be held for a short time. Thank goodness the notion that the badly trained inflexible divisions will not perform so well against the flexible NATO divisions has gone. Even if true, this is not the basis upon which the defence of Europe should be planned.

There are a number of ways in which the WP could attack NATO in West Germany. If such an attack did take place, it would have been carefully thought out and the risks considered. Let us therefore take one possible scenario. Assume that there is a limited political aim – the neutralisation of Germany. To achieve this the Soviets decide on a major, but limited attack into the northern half of Germany. In fact, they have selected what they know to be the boundary between the Northern Army Group (NORTHAG) and the Central Army Group (CENTAG). Their military commanders have been ordered to reach Bremen and Minden in three days. If they succeed, it is the Soviets' intention to stop then and offer to negotiate a political settlement involving the neutralisation, and signing of a non-aggression pact with, West Germany. When hostilities start, the Netherlands, Belgium and Denmark will all be informed of the limited aim of the aggression. The Russians also announce to the world a 'no first use of nuclear weapons'. This attack is carried out with very little military pre-preparations in order to give plenty of time for British and NATO political leaders to misread the initial signs.

The political intention is to weaken the resolve of the European NATO powers to raise the temperature by extending the conflict elsewhere. This might be achieved, by specifically undertaking to limit the hostilities to West Germany, to encourage Peace Movements in Denmark, Belgium and the Netherlands to take to the streets with a campaign of non-involvement. US major ground forces will not be engaged nor their existence threatened, thus the US President will have to take a decision to order nuclear release, not to ensure that US forces are not defeated conventionally, but to save European formations. The Russians could hope that his doubts will last three days.

NORTHAG has four army corps. Two of these, the Dutch and Belgian, are in the main stationed in their own countries. The overstretched German Corps in the initial stages therefore has some of its formations and units deployed to fill these gaps. Even if all the NORTHAG units were deployed, the military mathematics makes depressing reading. Against some thirteen to sixteen divisions, or division equivalents, will come an initial assault by about forty tank and motor rifle divisions. At the selected axis of advance of, say, five in the NORTHAG area a local superiority of between 5 and 7:1 will be achieved. Behind this first assault wave will be the 2nd Tactical Echelon of something in the order of another fifty divisions of which, let us say, thirty will be directed against NORTHAG whilst the others head south to maintain a visible military threat against CENTAG. This would be to discourage the move of any CENTAG reserves north.

THE BRITISH DIMENSION

What is likely to happen? Quite apart from the non-arrival of the Dutch and Belgian units, whose move forward will be impeded by air attacks, let us consider the problems facing the British Corps. This

Corps is not at war establishment. However, the initial deployment plans cater for units getting to the forward battle locations with their first line ammunition. However, war is not about well thought out plans. It is about blood, death, panic and chaos. Within the British Corps area are some 160 000 British non-combatants. Of these, thousands are families. Many children will be at the army boarding schools away from their parents. No one can honestly say that there would not be a rising tide of fear as rumours spread of the impending start of hostilities. How many fathers will put their families in their cars and make for the Channel ports to see them safe in their own country before returning to duty? What is the German reaction going to be as the autobahns fill with British cars with British families fleeing westwards? Can one rely on the Civil Servants and their families to conduct an ordered preplanned return to the UK or will it degenerate into every man for himself? It would only take one in ten of the soldiers in BAOR to think of, and act for, their families and many units' combat efficiency would be severely impaired in the initial stages.

Serious as these problems might be, there is one that is even worse. It concerns the Territorial Army. This can only be deployed on the signing of the Royal Proclamation. It is the TA which brings the British Corps up to war establishment. Many of the TA units are 3rd and 4th line units and it will be these units that are needed to move forward the bulk of the tank and artillery ammunition. Will they ever get there? If such an attack was launched, it will have been carefully planned. What then will be going on in the UK? Surely organised rioting, peace campaigns and the like will be arranged. Key installations may well be attacked. Deliberately fostered rumours of nuclear attack will be spread. It is likely that the police will not be able to cope. Nor will the Regular Army. The only other organised force in the UK, with its own transport, its own communications and internal discipline is the TA. Can one really see any Prime Minister allowing this force to leave the country in the circumstances outlined?

The effect on the British corps will not be immediately apparent. However, in holding the initial assault of the WP leading echelons, it will, almost certainly use up its 1st line ammunition. The rates at which tank and artillery, especially artillery, ammunition (both field and air defence) is expended are quite extraordinary. The Corps will simply run out of ammunition or, if conserving it, will be forced to withdraw – and units on the move immediately become vulnerable to air attack. As far as air defence missiles go, the total stocks held in

Germany might last for one, or at most two days, if the Soviet ground attack air attacks come in at the expected rates. This assumes, of course, that those missiles held in the ammunition dumps even reach the units.

All this time the nuclear regiments are in hiding and being guarded. Their presence at this stage is meaningless in tactical terms, except that, if the units concerned were armed with conventional heavy artillery, they may actually be of some use, whilst the battalions guarding the nuclear warheads could also be released for more productive work. In each NORTHAG Corps area, within 48 hours, all the divisions will have been committed. Behind them, nothing. The fact of the matter is that with the present level of regular divisions, a forward defence conventional defence is a fraud. Even if the numbers of NATO divisions were doubled there would still be a very large question mark over the defence capability of NATO ground forces. However, NATO does have powerful air forces in the Central Region. The two Allied Tactical Air Forces (2 ATAF in the north, 4 ATAF in the south) are now commanded by a single (American) Commander, COMAAFCE (Commander Allied Air Forces Central Region).

In the scenario postulated the co-ordinated air power of the whole of the Central Region would be directed against the WP ground and air forces. One of the main tasks that the army commander would want is for interdiction attacks against the WP reserve formations. However, WP air defences are sophisticated and numerous. The air battle would be of vital importance, particularly if the aggression has limited aims. It is the effectiveness of NATO air power directed against the WP reserve divisions that may well be decisive. In the end, the whole result might depend upon the time it takes NATO ground forces to run out of ammunition against how much delay NATO air power can impose in the forward movement of the WP reserves.

THE WEAKNESS OF THE BRITISH DEFENCE POSTURE

Our main concern, however, is for Britain's defence policy. At present the 1st British Corps performs the peace-time function of demonstrating commitment to NATO, by being where it is. However, a Central Region posture, if it is to make sense after deterrence fails, requires numbers. These we do not have. The most depressing aspect of all this is that this has been known for years and yet no UK Defence Minister has really risen to the challenge of facing the facts and proposing a more realistic defence policy. Fudging is still the order of the day. The point was made eleven years ago:

> The plain fact is that, once the immediate nuclear response has ceased to be the core of NATO's defence strategy, it must be replaced by the immediate deterrent value of strong land and air forces in being in the right place and in sufficient strength to be effective.[23]

Alone of the major European powers, the UK does not have National Service. As Britain's defence rests on nuclear deterrence, so large conventional forces were not needed. Flexible response, which requires large conventional forces, became NATO strategy within a decade of the Sandys 1957 White Paper. The point is that, alone of the European countries, we have no sizeable reserves. And, if the British Corps is lost, the UK will have lost the bulk of its army.

> It is now planned that the British [Corps] in Germany together with the other national forces will be required to fulfil a function not unlike that performed by the Old Contemptibles in 1914. It will be virtually destroyed.[24]

Buying time with blood makes some sense if there is a pool of National Servicemen to form the basis of a reserve army. Such a strategy makes no sense at all if all one has is a highly trained Regular Army. In fact, it does not actually make sense to anyone else, hence the introduction of battlefield nuclear weapons. However, as small armies with nuclear weapons will lose against large armies with nuclear weapons, the whole concept of actually fighting a nuclear battle in Europe is also pretty stupid. We therefore come back to the problem of what can realistically replace the Immediate Nuclear Response Strategy in the Central Region.

In the Southern Region, the problems of geography make a single scenario rather doubtful. Is it likely that a major campaign would be waged in eastern Turkey? That is in the NATO context. The juxtaposition of Yugoslavia, Albania, Bulgaria, Greece and Turkey produce an interesting political as well as military problem. Mobile military operations are likely to be restricted, if they ever take place, to the Macedonian Plain. The mobility of the Greek and Turkish armies is nowhere near the standard of those in Central Europe. Yet, certainly in the case of Greece, this can well be an advantage as the mountainous terrain lends itself more to guerrilla type infantry operations than the sort of more mobile operations anticipated in Germany.

However, British interests have virtually disappeared in the Southern Region of NATO. We do admittedly have the sovereign bases in Cyprus and a small naval presence. But our commitment to produce land forces is really restricted to providing contingents for the ACE (Mobile) Force. This is a NATO formation of brigade strength with contingents from a number of NATO countries. Its task is, by being deployed to an area of rising tension, to provide a visible sign of NATO's determination to resist aggression in that area. As a fighting force its capability is limited. The Southern Region is one area which NATO has a greater concentration of air power than the WP. The presence of the US 6th Fleet, which at some stage in the NATO alert procedures becomes a NATO force (Strike Force South), with its attack carriers, possibly two on station, can provide air support to augment that already in location.

This region is dominated by the sea and it is likely therefore that the issue will largely be decided at sea. Strategic surprise will not be so easy to achieve as, if the Soviets do intend to start hostilities, they will need to reinforce their Mediterranean squadron. This cannot really be done without NATO getting to know about it. Units of the Black Sea Fleet have to pass through the Bosphorus to get to the Mediterranean. It is not likely that reinforcement will be from the Northern Fleet. Not only will that have its own tasks, but the Straits of Gibraltar offer NATO an ideal surveillance choke point at which to observe the comings and goings of shipping going East and West between the Atlantic and Mediterranean.

THE PROBLEM IN THE NORTH

The Northern Region with its geographical peculiarities is also dominated by seas: the North Sea, the Norwegian Sea to the West and North, and the Skagerrak and Baltic in the south and south east of the region. Forward defence is difficult to achieve in strength on land. North Norway, arguably the most strategically important part of the region's land mass, is thinly populated. So the major problem facing NATO commanders is not just forward defence but the timely arrival of reinforcements. In the southern part of the region, Denmark's strategic geographic position, dominating as she does the exit from the Baltic to the North Sea, makes her a prime objective, either for a limited aggression or in the initial stages of a general war in Europe. The island of Bornholm, an ideal 'observation post' for NATO, could well be a test of NATO solidarity at some future date. How would NATO respond to the landing of, say, a marine brigade on Bornholm? Is the Soviet Union likely to honour the neutrality of Finland and Sweden?

Forward defence in the Northern Region must surely require the permanent stationing of ships in the NE Atlantic. An aggression against North Norway is likely to be from the sea or at the very least supported from the sea. The Soviets will need to neutralise the whole of the Finmark area if the Northern Fleet is to be able to deploy out of and back into Murmansk. NATO's problem is to identify the movements of the WP amphibious and naval units as being with hostile intent. As it is, there is a pattern of training exercises with these amphibious forces. One such exercise could very easily turn into something more. Ideally of course NATO reinforcements will have already arrived in north Norway before actual hostilities begin, but if they do not, what then?

Is the requirement for those forces to be able to fight their way ashore? Or are they to land further south and then to advance north? In either event have they the necessary support, air in particular, to enable them to engage an enemy who will have considerable land based air support? If air support is a necessity, from where will it operate? The Norwegian air bases are few and in any case cannot take significant reinforcements, as they do not have the logistics and maintenance facilities, despite the significant improvements that have been made in the last few years.

The UK commitment is to provide a commando brigade, reinforced by a Dutch marine battalion, plus RAF ground attack and other supporting aircraft. There are also contingencies for US marines and their supporting sea and air units to join in. Their problem will be to get across the Atlantic and, if hostilities have started, that is not going to be easy. Once hostilities have begun, SACLANT may well have higher strategic priorities than getting a few thousand US marines ashore in north Norway, which is actually not in his area of command responsibility.

In practical military terms, the Norwegians had better not place too much reliance on the US forces arriving. This leaves the UK reinforcements. They are well trained and now, since the Falklands, combat experienced to a level higher probably than any other comparable formation in NATO or the WP. The Falklands campaign has shown the level of support needed to project a brigade into combat against an opponent who has significant air power available.

In the Northern Region let us postulate that, at some time in the future, the Soviets calculate that they may be able to change the political environment by military means. They plan on amphibious landings at a number of points in the Finmark area to coincide with a limited assault across the Norwegian/Russian border. At the same time, amphibious and parachute landings are to take place at Spitsbergen and Jan Mayen. A submarine screen is deployed to patrol the seas between Greenland, Iceland, the Faroes, the Shetlands and Norway. Publicly the Soviets declare the limited aims of their military activities which they announce are necessary to secure their own strategic vital interests in the Kola Peninsula. Surface elements of the Northern Fleet including their carriers are also deployed to support their amphibious forces in all three tactical areas of operation. Iceland has been advised on pain of air attacks not to allow NATO forces to land.

The familiar campaign of self-justification is launched in the UN and through 'peace movements'. No first use of nuclear weapons is publicly announced in Moscow. The Norwegians ask for NATO to respond. If (Sir) John Nott's policies had continued there could be no response from the UK which could, in the scenario postulated, be militarily realistic. Even today well over two years after the Falklands campaign the commando brigade still has no organic area air defence system (the Rapier) as part of its order of battle. Soldiers and marines who experienced air attack in the Falklands at least knew that but for the Rapiers these attacks would have been worse. Now they train for war in north Norway and they see that there are no Rapiers. The fudging goes on. If the Norwegian air bases at Trømso and Bödö have been taken out the only timely air support that might be available will be from carrier borne aircraft. We have yet to increase our carrier capability.

THE MARITIME CONTEXT

In the Northern Region the key to the security of the region is the naval/air battle. Because of the terrain, numbers are not the factor in the land battle that they are in the Central Region. But small defending forces must have immediate air support. If the battle at sea is lost they will not have it.

A submarine oriented navy can be a strategic threat. Just one submarine can pose a significant deterrent effect on the operation of a naval force. However, what a submarine based navy cannot do is to support ground forces against air and ground attack. For this one needs a mix of surface ships including carriers. So no UK carriers, no UK amphibious capability for the Northern Region.

This battle will be fought by C-in-C EASTLANT, a British admiral under the operation command of SACLANT. Whether he will be allotted a US attack carrier task force one cannot tell. Much will depend upon what the situation is elsewhere. The US Navy itself is now able to conduct only a limited ocean war. This shortfall is taken care of, it appears, by the so-called swing strategy. Elements of the Pacific Fleet will reinforce the Atlantic Fleet if that is where the threat lies. This will take time. SACLANT, who, it must be pointed out, has a status in NATO equal to that of SACEUR, has repeatedly stated that the NATO navies cannot now fulfil their tasks. UK Defence Ministers have all (but the two most guilty are Healey and Nott) reduced the capabilities of the Royal Navy. That men appointed to this vital national office should so fail to understand that an island nation depends ultimately for its conventional defence on being able to secure the sea around is quite extraordinary.

The following quote from a lecture on the future of British maritime forces by Admiral Sir Henry Leach to the Royal United Services Institute on 9 June 1982 puts the problem of balance in perspective:

> When comparing the numbers of hulls on each side, the West still has numerical superiority in surface forces but the underlying trends show our numbers to be reducing whilst those of the Soviet navy are increasing. A year ago SACLANT assessed that on present trends the balance will tip towards the WP by the mid 1980s. Matters have hardly improved in our favour since then and some would argue that the balance has already tipped. *Remember it takes some 10 years to produce a new major weapon system or a ship* [author's emphasis]. Furthermore, although totting up numbers used to be a straightforward way of presenting relative strength when like was being compared with like, and the maritime problem was comparatively simple, technological advances of this century have changed the nature of war at sea beyond recognition. ... Again I believe people are sometimes misled by the accepted principle that, on land, to take the offensive you need a superiority

> of about 3:1. But at sea, the opposite applies and it is the defence that requires the numerical advantage, particularly for anti-submarine warfare in which a mix drawn from Maritime Patrol Aircraft (MPA), organic helicopters, surface ships and submarines is needed for success against a single nuclear submarine. At one time in 1943, 50 German submarines were being opposed by something in the order of 25 carrier types, 800 escorts and 1,100 MPA. The West cannot take comfort in parity, but needs a substantial superiority to defend our interest at sea, let alone carry the offensive to the enemy.[25]

He had previously made the point that the USSR has over 400 submarines!

Why for instance did Healey introduce the concept that the UK would not conduct offensive amphibious operations against a sophisticated enemy without allies? Once this became the (Labour) Government's policy, the demise of the British attack fleet carrier was certain. Yet, within a decade, we had to undertake just such an operation. *Ark Royal* by then was already in the breaker's yard. If she had been operational, the most serious gap in the task force, the total lack of long range early warning airborne radar, would have remained filled. It is not too fanciful to attribute the loss of every single British warship in the South Atlantic campaign to that decision by Denis Healey. If Galtieri had waited one more year, John Nott's defence policy, for which he received a knighthood – one of the most extraordinary honours ever awarded – would have ensured that the task force could not have sailed at all!

Now it is easy to say that the Falklands was a 'one off'. However, as Britain's vital interest in NATO is as much in the Northern Region as it is in the Central Region, the need for amphibious forces able to conduct offensive and defensive operations against a well armed opponent are as essential in the NATO context as in 'out of area' operations.

SPECIALISATION OF EFFORT

Flexible response does indeed require strong conventional forces. It requires, sea, land and air forces able to exert power at all points within the NATO boundaries. Obviously each NATO country has its own peculiar military contribution to make. These contributions are determined by the geographical position of each country and its particular industrial base. For instance, it is obvious that West Germany's contributions should be land and air forces, with only a limited naval contribution. Spain, the latest member, will be most useful to NATO in the provision of naval and air forces. The UK, owing to its particular geographical position, is, as it were, a halfway house between SACLANT and SACEUR. It provides a major NATO (MNC) commander (CINCHAN) as well as a major subordinate commander under SACLANT–CINCEASTLANT – and another two under SACEUR–CINCNORTH and CINCUKAIR. It provides naval forces in ACLANT as well as maritime air power and ground and air forces in ACE, as well as amphibious forces for SACEUR. Home defence, both land and air, also has to be provided for. This is too much. The jam is too thinly spread.

6 A Shift in Priorities

If we consider the three regions of the European NATO, there are two, the Northern and Central, where Britain's interests are immediately at stake. The Southern Region is a part of NATO, but the survival of the UK is not immediately threatened if, say, an invasion of Eastern Turkey takes place. Nevertheless the Southern Region, with its conflicts between Greece and Turkey, the continuing troubles in the Middle East and North Africa, make it a region where Soviet influence will be exercised to try to weaken NATO. In the Central Region there is an identity of interest which makes it difficult for the Soviets to divide the European NATO nations. Here their efforts will probably be concentrated in attempting to divide the people from their Governments, through the exploitation of Peace Movements and the playing on the natural fears of nuclear war. Anti-Americanism will be encouraged. However, it is in the Northern Region where the Soviets might think that they have the best chance, in peace-time, of splitting NATO.

The Scandinavian dimension is one which the USSR exploits today. The idea of a neutral 'non-nuclear' Scandinavian/Baltic Region is attractive and is pushed in some circles now. Already two of the Scandinavian countries, Sweden and Finland, are neutral and there are even voices in Denmark and Norway suggesting that particular path, despite the experience of both those countries in 1940. The sheer weight of Russian military power in the Kola Peninsula might, in time, persuade the Norwegians that their national interests could be better served in coming to an arrangement with their neighbours, along the lines of Finland, rather than staying in a NATO alliance, whose capabilities to reinforce and defend her begin to look less and less realistic as the Northern Fleet grows in power, whilst at the same time the US Navy and Royal Navy continue to be reduced by their respective governments.

The Central Region is able to look after itself. However, Britain's strategic position will be hopelessly undermined if the Northern Region became indefensible or if it broke up. Our major contribution to NATO's continuing solidarity would be better directed therefore in strengthening our contribution to the Northern Region. This will have to be at the expense of our present force levels in the Central Region. The Royal Navy which is, in a NATO context, the Eastern flank of the US Navy, must be strengthened, so that SACLANT is better able to maintain the link between the USA and Europe. Our amphibious forces must be given the visible capability of being able to respond, in strength, with a high probability of tactical success, to any threat posed by Soviet naval and amphibious forces in the region.

What then of the Central Region? The present conventional posture combined with a flexible response is incredible. If the British contribution of 1 (BR) Corps is removed or reduced clearly the strategy will become even less credible. What can be done? Too much time has been spent in tinkering with existing forces and their structure. Obviously the introduction of smart bombs, more effective anti-tank weapons, greater standardisation within NATO forces are all desirable but, as has already been said, no more Regular divisions will be forthcoming and that is what is needed, unless some other approach is adopted.

A NEW DEFENCE CONCEPT IN GERMANY

The Maginot Line concept has apparently been rejected. Yet this could be an answer. The Maginot Line itself was never breached. Its weakness was that it was not continued to the Channel. The Germans never went through or over it; they went round it. This weakness need not be repeated. The French reserves which still could have had a decisive influence were incorrectly placed, being deployed right up against the Maginot Line. If they had been deployed further back, they would have enabled the French High Command to have effectively redeployed them. This incidentally is a potential weakness in the forward defence posture – NATO reserves will be committed too early. Unfortunately, the Germans could react against producing a fortified frontier as it would solidify the division between the two Germanys. An example of politics entering into defence in Germany was the decision not to build the Elbe–Zeiten canal so that it represented a real tactical obstacle to WP forces. Although no straight answers were ever forthcoming, it was said that the decision not to allow the canal to be built with perpendicular sides was taken at a high political level. At the time, the early 1970s, the *Ostpolitik* policy was in vogue. As it is, as one cynic in a NATO HQ once said, it, the canal, now represents an obstacle to the Netherlands (NL) Corps but not to the Warsaw Pact. The strategic and tactical advantages that a major obstacle, such as a Maginot type defensive lane along the West German border, would have been immense. This sort of fixed defensive fortification could undoubtedly produce the 'pause' that NATO requires in any non-nuclear operations in the Central Region. It would also be well to the East, thus in fact reducing the conventional attack option by the WP into the Central Region to that of a complete non-starter, by ensuring that a quick tactical success was not possible. Thus even with an attack with little or no warning, this option would have ceased to be realistic. Thus the likelihood of any 'try on' in the Central Region would be reduced to a very low level of probability. The existing NATO forces, small though they are, would be more effective as a far larger proportion of them could be held back as mobile reserves thus providing the depth to the defensive system not there at present. One of the tasks of the Central Region tactical air forces will be of course to ensure that any concentration of WP formations, and they will be forced to concentrate to breach a well constructed defensive lane, would be ruthlessly attacked. But have the Germans the political will to construct such a defensive system?

A possible second solution is to consider a totally different form of non-nuclear defence for the Central Region. As NATO cannot, or will not, provide sufficient armoured and mechanised divisions then should it not look at the Swiss and Swedish concepts of defence? Would not a national militia provide a more formidable proposition? Instead of basing a conventional defence on too few normal divisions would it not be worth considering a defence based upon a 'nation at arms'? Every village, every town, every parish and street to have its own militia unit, armed and organised to fight in its own area.

One of the weaknesses of the present tactical concept in the Central Region is the situation with regard to the larger German towns and cities. Most of them are, one suspects, planned to be left virtually undefended or even declared 'open' cities. These, in the event of hostilities, would act as magnets to Warsaw Pact and Soviet forces. Of all nationalities, the Russians are aware as to how towns and cities can eat up armies. The German 6th Army was destroyed at Stalingrad, surely then Hamburg, Hanover, Bremen and others can provide formidable obstacles to a successful military takeover. With such a defensive concept, bolstered by mobile ground forces and powerful air forces, might not break-through cease to be an option?

West Germany would absorb an invasion like a sponge. Specially selected determined units of local militia, hiding up in woods and hills, having allowed the land units to pass, would fall upon the more vulnerable, softer targets – ammunition and supply trucks, headquarters and suchlike. Other units armed with short range anti-tank weapons would seek to 'kill' tanks. In this respect the North German plain of the 1980s is not the same as that of the 1950s. Ribbon town development has resulted in the countryside being much more of a mixture of town and country than thirty years ago. Tanks are vulnerable to infantry in hills, valleys, woods and streets. Gone are the days of the charge over the rolling plains. Towns and cities would become places to be avoided rather than entered. The recent fighting in the Lebanon has shown just how effective relatively small groups of determined men, armed correctly, can be against tanks in streets.

Such a concept will require a total rethink on the part of the military. Vast numbers of hand held anti-tank weapons will be required. The Germans already have the basis of a militia organisation in their two Territorial Commands, at present responsible for rear area security behind the two army groups. Such a form of defence might well appeal to many in Germany who at present avoid National Service on various grounds. It will have the immense advantage of being able to make effective use of reserve manpower up to the age of sixty. A nation of some 66 million ought to be able to produce a really formidable proposition to any future WP invasion. It would not be unreasonable to expect West Germany to be able to create such a force amounting to at least two million armed men.

Local units would not have to have sophisticated equipment except for their weapons. Transport could be civilian. Country units could make use of farm tractors and lorries while village and town units could use private cars or corporation buses. There would be no requirement for strategic mobility and indeed a minimum of tactical mobility will be needed. The idea would be that units would fight in and around their own homes or factories. Local knowledge of the byways, hills, valleys, woods, etc., would do a great deal to compensate for shortfalls in traditional military equipment.

Such a defence could be effective. Certainly the Russians are aware of just how much guerrilla forces can achieve behind the lines. The Yugoslavs held down large numbers of German troops out of all proportion to their own size. The deterrent value of such a defence would be at least the equal to the deterrent value of NATO's present Central Region strategy. Not only because of the problems such a militia would present to any invading force but because it would also enhance the value of the traditional NATO Corps.

A CHANGE IN BRITISH PRIORITIES

The British realignment of her ground forces to the Northern Region will have to be done in co-ordination with any new concept of defence in Germany. However, unless the UK actually begins to make the first move, nothing will happen. The endless talks about improvements to this weapon system, or that formation will go on. However, only a fundamental change in concept will get anything done at all.

The suggestion that Britain should withdraw from Germany or reduce its commitments there are always greeted with cries of horror from the Foreign Office, the Ministry of Defence, Central Front Lobbyists, and the Army. This suggestion is not, however, in any sense a withdrawal from NATO, nor should it be used as a vehicle for simply cutting the defence budget. This last is a major problem. A rationalisation of defence effort can too easily be used, by a Government under pressure to reduce expenditure, as an excuse for simply cutting costs in the area of withdrawal, without increasing expenditure in the areas where greater commitment is needed.

NATIONAL SERVICE

The Brussels Treaty commitments, so easily entered into, are not in the best interests today of either Britain or NATO. Western Europe is no longer an exhausted war-ridden group of poor states but a dynamic economic force in the world. West Germany is an ally firmly committed to NATO and an influential member of the European Economic Community (EEC). Britain's ability to maintain up to 55 000 men in Germany and at the same time to perform her other vital defence functions (home defence amongst them), whilst having only regular forces, will always mean that the forces are under pressure. Such a large commitment to the continent of Europe really only makes sense if we have National Service. Paradoxically the CND campaign has begun to highlight this problem and indeed the suggestion that the UK should reintroduce National Service has actually been mooted by some in CND. Those who made this suggestion are quite right. A strong conventional defence needs very large forces indeed. Whether or not the power represented by an army of, say, a million men is a deterrent in the same league as a Polaris submarine on station is the question to which they must produce an answer.

The forces themselves, in the view of most senior officers, would not welcome the return of National Service. The idea of the services, and the army in particular, becoming a vast training machine does not appeal. The argument is advanced that, with the sophistication of modern equipment, National Service would be too inefficient to produce the right answer. This is not necessarily true. The Royal Navy and Royal Air Force man equipment and their requirement is certainly for highly trained professionals. But the Army equips men and, as do all the major forces on both sides of the Iron Curtain, could in fact produce a pretty good answer with National Service, so long as the leavening of good long serving officers and NCOs is there. With its regimental system and peculiar discipline the British Army is actually more able to produce a well trained National Service army than most others.

When in 1957 the proposal by the then Conservative Government to end National Service was made, this was done in the context of nuclear superiority for the West. A war between NATO and the WP was therefore, it was considered, going to be short. This is no longer the case. That being so, why should National Service not be reintroduced? Even if the assumption, and a very convenient assumption it is, that any future war in Europe will be short is correct, Britain's lack of reservists who have done some form of military training is a source of weakness. Indeed, its consequence is such that Britain is unable to fight other than a short war. This must be corrected either by reintroducing National Service or by changing our whole defence policy. But is the country prepared to accept NS? More important, is any Government prepared to put the case to the country?

THE NEED FOR HONESTY

Unfortunately Britain has generals and military staffs that are too good. It is not new that politicians have demanded too much, in terms of commitments, and allowed too little in military resources. The problem has been the plans have been produced with too little, that might just work. Those contingency plans that have had to be activated have, in the main, produced the answers. One has only to look at the Falklands campaign, to examine the speed with which the task force was cobbled together, to consider the work involved in requisitioning merchant ships to see just how good the central staffs are at the Ministry of Defence.

That the task force actually succeeded in retaking the Falklands

Islands against a superior force, in numbers at any rate, which had had time to prepare its positions, with the relatively few casualties that it suffered was quite extraordinary, in pure military terms. It performed this despite having inadequate means which were due entirely to political decisions. The absence of *Ark Royal* and the vital gap that its absence left has already been alluded to. But this was not the only case of the force being equipped with weapons that were known to have poor performance. As Admiral Leach somewhat bitterly remarked in a speech to the RUSI: '[The Sea Dart's] performance in action has been entirely as expected. The planned improvements to correct its known shortcomings were cancelled as part of the [defence] cuts'.[26]

Now the services are, to some extent, to blame for this. Too few senior officers have been prepared to stand up and be counted when things are done as cost savings exercises, which are quite obviously wrong. The disgraceful saga of the vanishing brigade level of command in the army, in which this tactically vital level of command was removed, against the known views of virtually every field commander in Germany, is an example of intellectual fudging at a high level. In this particular case, British officers in NATO appointments, who questioned the tactical wisdom of the change were accused of disloyalty. Yet so obviously was the brigadeless division a military nonsense that today, less than seven years later, the Brigade Headquarters is back in the order of battle. Why did it happen? How could it happen? At the time, the (Labour) Government was demanding considerable savings from the defence budget. The army's aim, a very laudable one, was to retain barrels and reduce overheads. However, would it not have been better to have honestly faced the Government with the facts – reduce costs, reduce capabilities, so reduce commitments?

A recent example of fudging was in the artillery order of battle in 1 (BR) Corps. The medium regiments recently had the number of guns per battery increased from six to eight. However, guns need men to serve them, and in intense operations the sheer physical effort of unboxing, preparing and loading medium shells and their charges is considerable. Such an increase in barrels requires, if the batteries are to perform as they will need to perform, extra manpower. This was not forthcoming with the actual guns. There were noises about an extra manpower allocation at a later date. Another fudge! Obviously one can take the view that, as a war is most unlikely, it will not really matter. The problem is that, if the men see military fudging taking place, because it 'doesn't really matter' this attitude will eventually pervade their whole outlook on their chosen career.

The military life is very different in one major respect from those in civilian life. A doctor trains to doctor and actually does so, as do engineers, draftsmen and so on. A servicemen trains for war. He could spend all his service life training and never see active service. A Falklands, or Aden, or Borneo is experienced by very few in the services. Indeed, Major-General Moore was the first British officer of that rank to command a division in battle since Korea (1951–3). None of the divisional commanders in Germany in 1 (BR) Corps have any experience of armoured warfare for real. They cannot afford the attitude that it does not really matter. It does matter and for another reason. To take the eight-gun batteries for instance. They represent a certain element of power. On maps, on exercises and in plans they will be assumed to be able to perform as eight-gun batteries. The fact of the matter is that, on the day, they will not and, unless the army frankly faces its political masters with the truth about manpower and equipment, it will continue to find itself forced to provide for too many commitments with too few resources.

Really good units will, indeed must, have a sense of urgency about their training in peace-time on the basis that 'it might happen tomorrow'. In the case of 3 Commando Brigade and the two Parachute Battalions, their performance in the Falklands at individual and sub-unit level showed them to be better than 5 Brigade, although from all accounts the Gurkhas, if given the chance, would have possibly been their equal. 5 Brigade was unlucky in that it was not really a brigade at all. It was a headquarters with some units. In the 1960s, when it formed part of the 3rd Infantry Division, the ground force element of the Strategic Reserve, it was a brigade. That is to say it had the correct balance of units, armour, artillery, infantry, etc. But in 1982, it arrived in the Falklands to fight, with a mixture of units that had never even trained together! Yet there was in the UK a Light Brigade with all its units which could have been used!

As far as the Navy is concerned, it must have restored to it the means to carry out its traditional function of protecting the sea lanes. Its strategic task in NATO is to be able to maintain control over the North Sea, the Channel, the Western Approaches and the NE Atlantic. It must also retain the capability of deploying and supporting a land force ashore in a hostile environment. The Navy has for years, despite the fact that 3 Commando Brigade is part of its order of battle, had a somewhat ambivalent attitude towards the need for maintaining 'amphibiousity'. It may come as a surprise to the reader to know that the future of the gun as a ship's armament was in doubt. Many senior officers in the Navy saw no need for naval gunfire support. Thank goodness that the few prophets both in the Navy and the Royal Artillery, who provide the forward observers on the ground, kept the art alive. As it turned out naval gunfire was a major contributing factor in the land battle in the South Atlantic.

The northern flank role, if taken seriously, will require effective and relatively large amphibious forces. What is needed is not a few really expensive 'all singing, all dancing' amphibious ships, but more 'cheap and nasties'. The only organisation in the world that can afford expensive specialised amphibious shipping is the USMC. We should not attempt to emulate that excellent corps. But nevertheless hulls capable of carrying men and equipment do not have to be festooned with expensive gadgetry.

If the Royal Navy is to become more effective as SACLANT's eastern flank, a great deal more attention must be paid to the arming of the fighting ships. Ship for ship, class for class, the Soviets outperform in terms of firepower and range, all our classes of fighting ship. Comparisons, all unfavourable, have already been made between frigate types and aircraft carriers for instance. A hull is a weapons platform. It is of little or no use if it does not have either enough weapons, or weapons that are good enough for their anticipated tasks. Penny pinching savings forced on the designers by, ultimately, the politicians through the Treasury, are self-defeating. The Sea Dart is an example. Just one ship lost in the South Atlantic, because of successful air attack, the success of which was due to the known shortcomings of the Sea Dart, will have cost the country more than the whole of the improvement programme, which did not take place in order to cut costs. False economies in defence spending have always resulted in expensive disasters and yet they continue to be made. Economies in defence must only be made by reducing commitments. Indeed, the core message is that unless we are honest over defence we will never get it right. Politicians tend to seize upon the easy option. Here is where the services must be absolutely honest in their advice. It is no good telling a Defence Minister that a particular reduction in force levels, or the elimination of a weapons system on a ship will merely make the task more difficult. He will take the most optimistic view. If a ship for instance requires a certain performance from its weapons then anything less must be totally unacceptable. Ultimately men's lives are at stake. And this penny pinching goes right down to, for instance, supplying cheap foam mattresses which, in combat, produced thick pungent smoke which when set alight put lives at risk.

The security of the Northern Region is vital to the UK's strategic interests. The sheer magnitude of the Soviet defence effort enabling the USSR to exercise a visible and overwhelming presence in this region is evidence that they knew very well just how strategically important the whole region is. The door to Europe may well be the Central Region but the key to that door is the Northern Region. If the Soviets can, over a period of time, by a judicious mixture of political and psychological pressure, bolstered by a visible military presence of the right mix, achieve their aim of decoupling Norway and Denmark from NATO, the UK's position becomes precarious indeed. NATO's Central Region will have been outflanked and the military situation, if deterrence should fail, would be infinitely more fraught. How is it then, that, despite our great maritime traditional wisdom, we have committed ourselves to a Central Front strategy at the expense of a maritime one? Why did John Nott's 1981 White Paper turn out the way it did?

MISTAKEN PERCEPTIONS

There is a clue in a speech made at the RUSI on 14 July 1982 by Air Chief Marshal Sir Michael Beetham. In it he described the problem of matching resources to commitments. He said:

> it has been easy for us to develop tunnel vision, especially in the Central Region where NATO and WP forces stand, if not quite eyeball to eyeball, at least so close to one another that the confrontation and the possibility of military action instil an urgency of approach and earnestness of attitude that are difficult if not impossible to duplicate where distances do not press so closely. By this I am not implying that the maritime dimension is not vitally important, too. In any future conflict there would undoubtedly be considerable sea traffic to reinforce and to re-supply Europe from North America; we must keep our sea lines of communication open and we could expect substantial opposition from the Soviet surface and sub-surface forces. Both the Central Region and the Eastern Atlantic are vital to our security. The difficult question comes in determining where our priorities lie when we simply do not have the

> resources to do all we would like to do. It was this question which kept our heads down in Whitehall for much of last year (1981). With the strategic nuclear deterrent and the air defence of the UK being of the highest priority, it became a matter of making some adjustments to our contribution to either Central Region or Eastern Atlantic – we had to give emphasis to one rather than the other. It was not an easy dilemma for the Secretary of State for Defence, John Nott, to resolve but let me leave this thought with you.
>
> Despite the build up of Soviet maritime forces over the years, they have still not attained conventional superiority over NATO forces in the Atlantic. . . . It must be assumed, discounting the case of a nuclear preemptive attack against the US or sheer miscalculation on the part of the Soviet leadership, that the most likely objective of the Soviets in Europe would be political domination, territorial/industrial gains, or the destruction of NATO forces and bases.[27]

What is of interest is the total absence of reference to the north or Norwegian Seas. Can it be therefore that John Nott never seriously considered the threat to the UK through the Northern Region?

The assumption in the speech that equality of numbers in the maritime context is good enough flies directly in the face of naval experience. As Admiral Leach made clear just over a month earlier, in naval warfare it is the defence which needs the overwhelming numbers.

Naval strategists never make the mistake of assuming that a short war is a possibility. This notion which is one which is certainly put forward by some protagonists of the Central Front strategy flies in the face of history. If one plans for a short war then stocks of ammunition can be kept relatively low. Indeed if one assumes a short war all sorts of awkward questions never have to be answered. Reinforcement across the Atlantic for instance loses its importance in the context of a seven day war. The problem is that

> any strategy which weakens NATO's capacity to reinforce across the Atlantic will inevitably lower the nuclear threshold, and unless a viable reinforcement capability is discernibly maintained the United States will not forward-deploy forces, especially ground forces to maintain Europe. Decoupling of the US is a prime Soviet aim. We must keep options open and avoid committing ourselves to an assumption which, if proved false, would be disastrous.[28]

CONTINENTAL OR MARITIME?

Here then is the fatal weakness of the Central Front strategy as it affects the UK. We have adopted a defence posture which is only relevant in the event of a conventional attack in that region. The British Army of the Rhine is quite useless for any other role except for individual units being taken out for specific small operations as they are at present for Internal Security duties in the UK. The point is that a maritime based strategy is relevant whatever form of attack takes place against NATO, whether it be in the Northern, Central or Southern Region or all three, whether it is in the form of naval operations in the Indian Ocean or South Atlantic, or even if it is in the form of politico-military pressure by the visible demonstration of power, say, by the Northern Fleet against Norway's continued membership of NATO. Most important of all it is relevant in a protracted war which, with the ammunition stocks available, is anything over ten days.

Quite apart from the advantages accruing to NATO if its military contribution to the defence, in peace-time, of the Northern Region, the resulting shortfall effect of conventional forces in the Central Region can be reduced by a redeployment of the existing formations in Germany. One of the potential problems is the fact that the US ground forces are deployed in the southern half of West Germany. But the most likely threat facing the region is a major attack in the NORTHAG area, presumably with the aim of reaching the Channel ports, thus cutting off NATO's continental forces from major sea-borne reinforcements. A redeployment of effort by the UK from the Central Region northwards could be matched by a similar shift by the moving of one of the US Corps into the NORTHAG area. In political terms, this would mean that any attack into the region, even if limited, would mean that major US ground forces would be committed with all that is implied therefrom. In military terms it would ensure that the shortest routes to the Channel and the Ruhr are still covered by significant NATO formations.

A BRITISH ROLE IN GERMANY

As the politics of defence are obviously important, the 'political' role at present performed by 1 (BR) Corps can just as well be fulfilled by the presence of a British armoured division. This should be established at virtually war establishment. The scales of ammunition should be kept at a much higher level than they are at present. In fact by not reducing the scales at present allotted to the Corps, such a division would be a formidable source of power in the hands of CINCENT as a mobile armoured reserve. The number of artillery units should, in relative terms, be increased. One of the weaknesses in the present order of battle of the (BR) Corps is its scale of artillery to armour and infantry. It is extremely poor and follows a pattern which unfortunately appears to be almost inevitable. In war, which has to do with the application of military power, artillery takes its rightful place as a major arm. In peace, when a generation of officers again appears that has not experienced combat, manoeuvre begins once more to become the means of winning battles (exercises). So the ratio of artillery to armour and infantry falls, until the next war comes along. Hence, if this error is not to be repeated, there is a requirement for a supporting artillery division to remain, thus giving to the armoured division the level of firepower that it will need if it is to perform its function as a hard hitting Central Region reserve. If deterrence fails and it ever had to be used and its role was indeed that of a mobile reserve, it would be committed when many other NATO formations will have been reduced by attrition. It will not be able to rely on the fire support of any other NATO formation and so must have sufficient of its own.

The inflexibility, in strategic terms, which the present deployment of the (BR) Corps imposes on the UK does not apply to the Royal Air Force. Air power has an inherent flexibility because of what it is. Thus, whatever strategy is adopted, whether Central Front or flexible maritime, those RAF units deployed in Germany as part of 2 ATAF should remain. Indeed, following the redeployment of land forces, there is a case for increasing the UK contribution to RAF (Germany).

SACEUR is able to reallocate air resources in the event of a period of rising tension or actual hostilities with a speed and flexibility not possible with his land forces. The performance of aircraft in their particular role is not too affected by the geographical position from which each starts its mission. Cross servicing facilities, which is one area in which NATO and the UK should continue to pay attention gives even more flexibility to the use of airpower. Cross servicing is the means by which an aircraft of one NATO nation can be rearmed and serviced after a mission, having landed at an airfield different from that from which it took off. Ideally any NATO aircraft of whatever NATO nation should be able to land at any other NATO airfield to be serviced. Obviously, this ideal may never be reached but nevertheless there is a requirement for similar aircraft to have this facility. This is of course a major strategic reason for the joint production of aircraft, quite apart from the sharing of development costs, a good enough reason, one may feel, for joint production anyway. It is also important that the UK and NATO agree on common weapon systems.

THE POLITICAL CONTEXT

In the political arena a potentially dangerous situation is beginning to arise in relations between Europe and the US and between individual European countries. This has to do with the EEC and the damaging effect that relationships within this organisation may begin to have in the defensive system in Europe. The two major organisations upon which Western Europe has based its future are NATO and the EEC. Unfortunately there are significant differences not only in the structure of the two organisations but also in their general outlook. There are stresses that are beginning to become apparent between the US and EEC.

NATO is more than a military alliance, although the Military Committee is the most prestigious of all the NATO committees. It is an international organisation and each member country retains absolutely its own sovereign independence. Regardless of decisions or proposals taken in the NATO councils, member nations retain the sovereign right to follow in full or in part, or indeed not to follow at all, any NATO proposal. A case in point is that of France which remains a full member of the alliance despite ceasing to be a participating member of the peace-time military structure.

The EEC on the other hand is a supra-national organisation. Member nations have, for good or ill, given up an element of their sovereignty as part of the price for joining the Community. The Community actually has the power to pass legislation binding in the courts of member states. It is able to deal with non-EEC countries on a decision-making basis. In trade for instance Japan has a relationship with the EEC and not just relationships with the individual EEC members.

The first area of conflict can be seen in the memberships of the two alliances. Of the two European NATO countries which have borders with Russia, Norway and Turkey, neither is in the EEC. Nor is the latest member of NATO, Spain. The most powerful member of

NATO, the USA, is not in the EEC, and not only that but is, arguably, the economic power most likely to enter into financial and trade conflict with the EEC. France has withdrawn from the NATO peacetime military structure, yet is one of the most influential, as well as an original, member of the EEC.

The perspectives of the two organisations are different and are in certain respects opposed to each other. NATO is concerned with the strategic view. This by its nature has to do with defence. Policies which may have the effect of strengthening the Soviet Union in the defence field are therefore against NATO's interest. Unfortunately NATO as an organisation can really only propose; individual countries ultimately make their own choice. The EEC is concerned with economics. It may therefore be less concerned with the long term strategic results of a particular policy than with the short or medium term economic results of a policy. The European–Siberian gas pipeline is a case in point. From NATO's perception any form of dependence for a source of power upon the USSR is not a good thing, while the EEC may well consider that cheap power is good no matter from whence it comes.

The USA has certain views on the export of 'strategic' goods to the USSR, yet this has caused strife between European countries and the USA. These strains are not good for Europe. They are not good for US–European relationships and, unless the sources of these strains can somehow be reconciled, there might be, in the long term, a permanent degradation of NATO–US–EEC relations which will be in no one's interests, except for the WP. The United Kingdom therefore should begin the process of devising policies to meld these two organisations together, in the long term interest of the West. The strength of NATO is that it does take a long term view of the strategic relationships between itself and the USSR. The EEC has the constitutional power actually to do something in strategic terms but, in fact, does not. A case in point is the situation with regard to the merchant fleets of the EEC. In strategic terms the continual reduction of the Western nations' merchant ship tonnage is extremely dangerous. Individual NATO countries could take national action. However, if the EEC was to take action by, say, requiring a minimum percentage of imports and exports to be carried in EEC flagships, this would go some way to redress the balance between Western national carriers and the Soviet merchant fleet, which is not constrained by economic considerations. Nationally the UK Government must take positive steps to stop the decline in the size of the national flag merchant service. The Falklands campaign could not have taken place except for the chartering by the Ministry of Defence of a large number of British merchant ships.

THE MERCHANT MARINE

In war, the UK will not be able to depend either upon foreign carriers or upon foreign seamen. Despite the present (Conservative) Government's dislike, on political grounds, of subsidy, for good sound strategic reasons, if subsidy is the only way in which a viable national merchant fleet can be kept in being, then that is what will have to be done.

It would obviously be better if such a policy became an EEC agreed method of maintaining a Western European merchant service, but until such an EEC policy does emerge then the UK needs to act, and act fairly quickly. The subsidising of shipbuilders to build merchant ships for Warsaw Pact countries is an exercise in crass stupidity which must not occur again. The same ships built for Poland with massive UK state aid could have equally been built for British carriers. We must, if necessary, be prepared to run a national merchant fleet at a financial loss and if necessary this loss, which is a strategic cost, could be accounted for in the Defence budget.

The same goes for the UK fishing fleet which has shrunk to a desperately small level. There are contingency plans for the Royal Navy to use trawlers as mine counter measure vessels. If the British fishing fleet continues its current rate of decline, these contingency plans will exist on paper only. Here the EEC fishing policy is acting in direct conflict with British strategic interests and, in fact, against NATO's interests too, as Britain, alone of the European NATO powers, is the key to the security of the Western Approaches, Channel and North Sea.

THE DANGER OF CONFLICTING INTERESTS

Clashes of national interest are more serious in the EEC than in NATO. The reason is that, being a supranational organisation, the EEC is able to compel its member countries, on pain of sanctions, to toe the line. Such compulsion must be through the due constitutional processes within the Treaty of Rome. Thus conflicts within the EEC, impinging as they do on the sovereignty of nations, are bound therefore to be extremely bitter. The Athens Summit (December 1983) is an example. Both Britain and France were determined that their own national interest would not be sacrificed to the common benefit. Such confrontations do the Common Market no good at all, but the potential damage to international relations within Europe, that these EEC disputes have between European countries might, in time, spill over into NATO. This would be a disaster; so indeed would be bad EEC–USA relations for the same reason. The long term strategic aim therefore for the UK is for the melding together of NATO and the EEC. In the meantime the UK should press for a system of formal relations to be set up between NATO and the EEC. Somehow the advantages of a strategic common outlook combined with individual national sovereignty (the NATO concept) with the economic and political strength of a supra-national organisation (EEC) must be synthesised. Possibly, with its global outlook, its military experience and geopolitical position, the UK is the one to start this exciting development.

SOME MILITARY SPIN-OFFS FROM A MARITIME STRATEGY

The central theme, however, is the switch of emphasis by the UK from the Central to the Northern Region for sound strategic reasons. The most visible sign of such a change in strategic posture will of course be the move of a number of army formations at present stationed in Germany back to the UK. If it is assumed, for the sake of argument that two divisions are moved and reassigned to their new roles, this would ensure that not only would the defence of the Northern Region become visibly stronger and more realistic, but the UK would at the same time immediately improve her 'out of area' capabilities. A light brigade, equipped and trained, to fight on foot, or with helicopters is a great deal more flexible in strategic terms than an armoured brigade in Germany. A helicopter trained brigade could indeed have a role in Germany. The West German Army has a number of Jaeger brigades, equipped with helicopters. Their units are used in fast moving anti-tank operations. The helicopter as a battlefield weapons platform, or troop carrier, has a tactical mobility performance far greater than either APC borne infantry or tanks.

The concept is that these units are moved to deployment areas in front of an aggressor's breakthrough where, with their high number of anti-tank missiles, they will 'seal off' the anticipated exploitation. British brigades stationed in the UK can very well be trained in this type of mobile operation which will be valid in West Germany, Jutland and, to a certain extent, in Norway. The type of training that such a brigade would undergo for this type of role will fit it for an unforeseen emergency outside the NATO area. Where else can an armoured brigade equipped with Challenger tanks, costing £1.5 m each, operate except in Germany?

THE UNSEEN FLANK

The strategic southern flank to NATO is not the Southern Region but the South Atlantic. Here NATO's maritime forces operate as national rather than NATO forces. Yet the security of the South Atlantic is of vital importance. Some 4000 ships pass the Cape of Good Hope from the Indian Ocean to Europe every year.

Plans exist on a national or bilateral basis for the conduct of naval operations in the South Atlantic. The main problem is surveillance. Here the Falkland Islands assume an importance which up till now has been ignored. The 'Fortress Falklands' policy can be justified not so much in keeping Argentina at bay, but in the creation of a facility which, in conjunction with those at Ascension Island and Silvermine in South Africa, will ensure that anti-submarine operations can be mounted throughout the South Atlantic.

The strategic importance of this 'unseen flank' was highlighted in the Omega Report, where it was described as being 'represented by the invisible economic lifelines to Africa, the Middle and Far East necessary to maintain Western European economic growth and independence'.[29]

7 The Nuclear Question

Once the first nuclear bomb exploded, a totally new influence was brought to bear, not only on military strategic thought, but also on the political relationships between the so-called superpowers. There is not much profit in looking back as to why the Americans used the two atomic weapons on Japan, nor in delving into the motives of those governments which have acquired a military nuclear capability since 1945. The facts are that, in the mid-1980s, there are a number of powers with significant nuclear capabilities. These range from the two major nuclear powers, the United States and the Soviet Union, to the United Kingdom with its mixtures of 'UK built' and 'US–UK' built systems, France with its own nationally built and independent *force de frappe*, China and India, both of whom have exploded their own weapons, and, in the background, it is probable that Israel and South Africa may have their own nuclear military capability. There are other countries which, if they do not have nuclear weapons, have the industrial and technological capacity to produce, in time, nuclear weapons if they were so minded.

BRITAIN'S DECISION TO GO NUCLEAR

Nuclear power in the military context justifies itself on its deterrent value. Defence and deterrence are different. It is the failure on the part of many people and pressure groups to appreciate this, which has led, in part, to the clouding of the nuclear issue and the place that it has, or ought to have, in the UK's overall strategic posture. After 1945, when the United States decided to stop the close level of cooperation which had existed between Britain and America in the design and production of the original weapons, the Manhattan Project, the then Labour Government decided that the UK should go ahead with the production of its own nuclear weapon.

At the time Britain was perceived, by herself certainly and possibly too by others, to be a Great Power. Whether this perception at the time was right or wrong is beside the point, the fact is that, because of this perception, Britain became, together with the Soviets, who exploded their first weapon in 1949, a nuclear power. Today she is still a military nuclear power.

Britain's nuclear policy must only really be considered within the context of her membership of the North Atlantic Treaty Organisation. There can be no unilateral nuclear policy by any nation with NATO at the expense of the other members if that nation is to continue to play its full part in maintaining the strength of the Alliance. However, inside the Alliance, there is plenty of scope for each country to have its own specific nuclear posture. For example in NATO there are nuclear and non-nuclear powers. Amongst the non-nuclear powers there is a variety of nuclear policies. Norway for instance, whilst subscribing to NATO's overall nuclear strategy, does not allow the deployment of nuclear weapons in her territory in peace-time. Western Germany, also a non-nuclear power, but with the capability of becoming one although treaty obligations prevent this, sees that an essential part of her contribution to NATO includes the deployment of US and NATO nuclear weapons on her soil in peace-time. Greece and Turkey, non-nuclear powers without a foreseeable chance of being able to produce their own nuclear capability, also allows US nuclear weapons to be deployed in peace-time within their borders.

On the other hand, the French do not permit NATO or US nuclear forces to deploy in France or in her territorial waters. However, France is a nuclear power in her own right. We then have the UK, which not only has her own nationally commanded and controlled nuclear forces but she has also agreed that US nuclear weapons can be stationed in the UK in peace-time. It so happens that US nuclear forces have been deployed in the UK for over 20 years and the agreement betweeen the two countries, which has been maintained by successive British and American Governments, whether Labour or Conservative on the one hand and Democratic or Republican on the other, has stood the test of time. It is of course reviewed by each incoming President and Prime Minister during their briefing periods on taking office.

Nuclear weapons cannot be disinvented. Policies which have been developing over some 35 years cannot be dismissed as irrelevant or unnecessary. NATO, as an Alliance of independent nations, arrives at its overall strategic policies by means of painstaking negotiation. There is no dictatorship in the councils of NATO. Instant solutions are not possible. Before embarking on a radical change in such a fundamental area as nuclear deterrence and nuclear backed defence, hard questions have to be asked.

Unfortuntely in the whole defence debate there are some who

advocate policies on nuclear matters for the UK as if either NATO did not exist. They imagine that any change in policy, which would seriously affect NATO's overall position, would be immediately accepted by the whole Alliance without question. Britain's nuclear policy cannot be considered in isolation. A specific case in point is the debate on the deployment of the Cruise missiles in the UK. Many unilateralists appear to take the view that Cruise is purely an American system deployed to further US interests. This is not so. Each cruise missile deployed in the UK is as much part of Denmark's defence as it is of the UK's. A unilateral decision by the UK to get rid of Cruise would weaken NATO's deterrent posture. Thus, within the Alliance, such a decision will inevitably weaken rather than strengthen the UK's position.

THE NEED FOR DEBATE

However, all this having been said, clearly there is a need for a continuing dialogue within NATO, because no policy should be allowed to solidify. If any NATO country believes that a particular strategy is wrong or can be improved upon, it must, by means of debate and presentation, seek to take the rest of the Alliance with it. It may well be therefore that the UK might come to a view about NATO's nuclear policies and its own role within those policies. If it then becomes clear that the vital interests of this nation require a change in its general defence policy such a change, if the Alliance is to remain strong, must be done after debate and with, hopefully, the agreement of the Alliance. However, if it becomes necessary for Britain to undertake a fundamental change in her strategic posture and she feels strongly that such a change will not only be in the interests of herself but would also, by strengthening her own defensive position, be in NATO's interests, it could be that, in these circumstances, she would have to proceed on such a change without the agreement of her NATO allies. Such a course of action would have extremely serious consequences. This would be so particularly if the changes were perceived by her NATO partners to be at their expense. This is why the naive isolationist approach of some CND protagonists over the question of Cruise is mistaken. The idea that somehow the UK can isolate itself from the East/West confrontation by removing all nuclear weapons from its soil and yet remain a member of NATO is quite plainly nonsense.

Nevertheless questions need to be asked, indeed should be asked. NATO's policies must be examined and re-examined, particularly in the nuclear field as this area is fundamental to NATO's whole defensive strategy. What then is NATO's strategic concept? The essence of NATO's posture is peace and security through strength. Whilst remaining free and independent nations, each member has nevertheless undertaken to regard an attack on any one member as an attack on all. First and foremost the NATO strategic concept is one of deterrence. That being so it has developed a nuclear strategic posture based, it must be said, on the nuclear power of the United States. This posture has been agreed to as a result of the usual processes of debate and staff work in various NATO committees, one of which is the Nuclear Planning Group.

What is Deterrence?

What then is the nature of deterrence? On the basis that nuclear weapons are a deterrent, is it desirable, or even necessary, to have as many as there are on the one hand, and, even if it were, does the Alliance really have to have the variety of delivery means that it has? These range from submarine based Poseidon missiles, able to reach any part of the world's land mass, to land based intercontinental ballistic missiles. These are based in the USSR and USA with the capability of hitting the heartland of either country. There are nuclear warheads which can be delivered by aircraft, as well as nuclear mines which can be dropped from helicopters. In Europe, on both sides of the Iron Curtain, land based medium and short range nuclear rocket forces are deployed and, with the shortest range of all there are nuclear shells able to be fired from ordinary medium or heavy artillery pieces.

One of the arguments deployed by some is that even if one accepts that nuclear deterrence is a reality, then this can be equally as effective with far less numbers than exist at present. 'There is no point in wiping out each other seven times, once is enough', the argument runs.

It is fair, however, to make the point here that NATO has in fact taken action to reduce the level of her nuclear stock-pile. 'Thus it was that surveys conducted by the High Level Group of the (NATO) Nuclear Planning Group (NPG) led to the decision made in 1983 in Montebello, Quebec, to again considerably reduce NATO's theatre nuclear weapons in Europe.'[30]

Another fear which has been expressed, particularly during the period immediately before the arrival of the first Cruise missile into the UK, is that some weapons, Cruise among them, are not deterrent weapons at all but nuclear war-fighting weapons. What lies behind these thoughts is the fear of a doctrine developing that fighting and winning a nuclear war is possible. Indeed, it is now being suggested that the Americans are going down this particular path and that their NATO allies will be pulled along with them.

These arguments are essentially false and betray a lack of understanding as to the nature of deterrent strategy where 'Flexible Response is in the final analysis a strategy of deterrence based on a close linkage or continuum of the conventional, tactical-nuclear and strategic-nuclear force components'.[31]

It so happens that other strands of political influence also enter the arena. One of the major problems in the nuclear debate is the probability that some groups, such as the Communists, who have certain long term political aims, the destruction of NATO, for example, will use spurious arguments, with the intention of discrediting nuclear deterrence, as a means of achieving those other long term aims. An example is the debate over 'dual key' for the Cruise missiles. When the CND raise the matter of dual key it is not because they would find Cruise more acceptable but, by raising quite needless fears in the minds of those who believe in the concept of nuclear based deterrence, they hope to discredit the system in principle. Others, and, it must be said, some are senior members of the Labour party, have quite openly exploited anti-Americanism to their own ends. Eventually therefore it is necessary to cut through all these various influences to get to the core of the nuclear argument.

Is nuclear deterrence real? Has the fact that there has been no armed conflict in Western Europe over the past 38 years, the longest continuous period of peace in Europe for over six hundred years, been the result of nuclear deterrence or is this coincidence? Even supposing that nuclear deterrence has been effective in the past, have we reached a point where the sheer magnitude of the overall nuclear destructive power possessed by both sides is itself becoming a destabilising factor? In other words have we passed through a period of effective deterrence to a 'post-deterrence' phase? What is the role of the non-super nuclear power? Is it significant that, whereas in the Warsaw Pact there is only one nuclear power, the USSR, in NATO there are three, the USA, UK and France? Does this multiplicity of decision-making centres in NATO contribute to deterrence or, by introducing uncertainty in the minds of the Soviet leaders, make the possibility of a general reduction in the level of nuclear stocks less likely?

Does unilateral disarmament have a place in deterrence strategy? Is the aim of deterrence merely to ensure that conflict between the major nuclear powers remains at a lower level than war, or is it, or should it be the reduction of all levels of nuclear weapons while maintaining an effective deterrent strategy? Nuclear weapons are here to stay. It is obviously unrealistic to imagine that they can all be destroyed and certainly the capability of manufacture remains. Nevertheless it is questionable whether, even if the level of nuclear weapons could be reduced to zero, the world would be safer. Part of deterrence and defence is non-nuclear. A problem here is that, in Europe, there is an enormous imbalance of non-nuclear forces in favour of the WP. There comes the point nevertheless when nuclear deterrence and the role of conventional forces in deterrence have to be seen as part of the same equation.

THE ROLE OF NON-NUCLEAR FORCES

The influence that conventional forces play in the nuclear posture of any country is one which possibly has not been examined closely enough. This is particularly so in the UK where, despite the fact that the main weight of the UK defence budget is directed towards its NATO commitment, the forces of the Crown have been engaged on active service ranging from major conventional land combat (Korea) to various levels of conventional all arms combat (Falklands, Suez, Borneo, Aden) to internal security operations (Cyprus, Northern Ireland) as well as short duration intervention missions (Kenya, post-independence). The point is that the strength of the UK's conventional forces has, over the years been reduced, yet this reduction has not been in sympathy with the actual level of commitments. The cost of a national nuclear deterrent force is high, not so much in money terms but in the diverting of skilled manpower and equipment from the level of conventional forces. This delicate balance between the nuclear and non-nuclear force levels that the UK can afford is a major problem and it has not yet been resolved. It is also a fact that every single operation in which the UK has engaged, with the exception of the internal security operations within the United Kingdom (Ulster), has been outside NATO's geographical boundaries.

IS DETERRENCE A REALITY?

Although deterrence has been a major concept in human affairs there appears to have been little study into what it is. '... from discussions with policy makers in the Pentagon, it is clear that there has been no adequate exploration of the nature of deterrence.'[32] Much of the literature on the subject of deterrence is NATO–WP orientated and bipolar in concept. One of the problems in dealing with deterrence theory is that many of the factors, psychological, geopolitical and so on may well be inaccessible to the analyst. How does one know a decision maker's intentions or the strategic evaluations that are being made by policy planners of a potential enemy, or actual enemy for that matter. Deterrence is not only to do with observable capability but with the mind of the opponent. To deter one has to first know one's own mind. It is then vital that one's opponent then also knows it. The recent classic case of deterrence failing was over the Falklands. On the one hand British Foreign Office desk officers made their assessments of likely Argentine moves in the light of their own perceptions. They were reasonable men. They assessed the situation. They no doubt assumed that the Argentine Government was run by reasonable men. The British military capability was clear for all to see and it is probable that the British military advice was that an Argentine invasion was not on. On the other side the Argentines had been dealing for years with a British Foreign Office which seemed to be giving signals that Her Majesty's Government would be happy, in the long term, to see the Falklands passing to Argentina. Mendes's perception of any likely British reaction was no doubt influenced by his dealings with Lord Carrington, who, when warned by Israeli intelligence that an invasion was going to take place refused to believe it, and when coming out of the Cabinet meeting, called immediately after the invasion, was still convinced that Britain would not go to war over the islands. The proposed paying off of *Endurance* in John Nott's White Paper in 1982 on grounds of economy was almost certainly the misread signal to the Argentines that Britain was not serious over the Falklands. Neither side understood the mind of the other, an essential ingredient of deterrence, resulting in a short bloody war demonstrating to the world the high cost of a failure in deterrence. John Nott's economy measure must be one of the most expensive misjudgements made in recent times.

Nuclear deterrence cannot be allowed to fail. In one sense, however, the arguments are more simplified in the nuclear context.

> The concept of deterrence was not born with the nuclear age; it has long been a part of international politics. Countries have always tried to induce fear in an adversary or at least to create strong doubts about the outcome of any possible aggression. ... The introduction of nuclear weapons potentially changed this situation because it simplified the calculations.[32]

Yet even this comment is open to question. It may well be that two nuclear powers may deter each other from direct military confrontation. But it is clear that a non-nuclear power is not deterred from engaging in military operations against a nuclear power (Falklands, Vietnam). Nor are resistance movements inhibited (Afghanistan) from taking on nuclear powers. It may well be therefore that nuclear deterrence is limited in its scope, indeed it is even possible that an aggressive minded power becomes less inhibited in its military adventures because the threat of provoking its major strategic (nuclear) rival has diminished. To be specific, would not the US be prepared to confront the Russians in East Africa, say, if nuclear weapons did not exist? The use of surrogate nations, Cuba in Africa, Syria in Lebanon, Libya in the Mediterranean, to further Russia's long term aim of general destabilisation makes it difficult for the US to contain Russian expansionism, because she is inhibited in the level of power that she can exert. Is it possible to conclude therefore that nuclear based deterrence is limited in its scope to affecting only those nations that either have nuclear weapons or belong to alliances which base their strategic military/political posture on, ultimately, a nuclear deterrent? This is relatively simple to postulate in the case of NATO, from NATO's point of view. NATO perceives itself to be defensive. It only has one threat, that of the USSR and the Warsaw Pact, and has stated that it will not initiate war, but that, if war does start, it might be forced to fire nuclear weapons; first if necessary. This is essentially the posture of deterrence. And taking the premise that peace has been maintained between West and East Europe for over 30 years, because of NATO's nuclear capacity, it has been, and still is, effective.

Within NATO there is little official debate upon the correctness or otherwise of NATO's basic deterrent policy. For example in two White Papers on the defence of West Germany the Netherlands 1984 paper states baldly 'There are no alternatives for the present strategy, which is based on nuclear deterrence'. The UK White Paper with a total of 517 paragraphs devoted only one to the discussion on strategy. 'We believe that this strategy remains the basis of a credible deterrent, and there is no better alternative available.'[34]

Would such a deterrent doctrine stop Libya for instance indulging in some military adventure at the expense of NATO? What if Libya was supplied with an Exocet Mk II system and decided to have a go at the US 6th Fleet? Is the deterrence here nuclear, or would it in this case rest on the observed conventional capability, of both defence and attack, of the American Fleet?

Certainly the problem of the limits of nuclear deterrence was foreseen as early as 1956. A direct quote from Michael Mandelbaun's *The Nuclear Question* makes the point:

> Kaufmann conceded that the threat of massive retaliation probably did deter a direct attack against the territory of the United States, or against areas that have come to be regarded as of vital interest to us. But we foresaw other contingencies that the Great Deterrent would not cover. He predicted that the Soviet Union and the People's Republic of China would push into peripheral areas not only for gain but for the purpose of discoverying what constitutes the limits of our tolerance.[35]

The point is later made that Korea and Indochina were two such peripheral areas. How does, or ought, this affect the UK nuclear policy? This country is a member of NATO. At present its nuclear forces are assigned to that alliance and have two sets of targets – one as part of a NATO plan and the other a purely national plan. Does NATO need the UK nuclear contribution? Beside the US forces is it a significant addition to the alliance arsenal?

THE EUROPEAN DIMENSION

Arguments are put forward that NATO's overall deterrent posture is strengthened by having some NATO European powers with their own nuclear weapons. More than one decision centre must complicate the calculations that the Russian leadership might have to make if they were ever to decide to change by military means the existing political situation in Europe.

It has sometimes been mooted that the British and French nuclear forces could form the basis of a European nuclear force on the basis, presumably, that this would be more in keeping with the 'European spirit' than two separate nationally controlled forces are. However one must suspect that, in part, the motivation behind the maintenance of European nuclear forces is the thought that, if the Europeans are entirely without some nuclear forces of their own, the US and USSR could come to some form of agreement in the future which might not be in the best interests of European defence. This is of course to do with trust and credibility of the Americans in the long term. This worry is probably at the back of the minds of all European leaders and concerns, not only the credibility that the US Strategic Forces have in the minds of the Russians over, say, the response to a minor incursion by the WP into NATO, but also as to the possibility of an Arms Limitation Agreement by the US and USSR at the expense of Europe.

> SALT raised in many minds a number of questions, both political and miltiary. One set of questions concerned the effects on the credibility of the American deterrent of the formal ratification of strategic parity and, as a corollary, the implications for future Soviet behaviour, with some of the Allies worried lest the Soviet Union might feel freer to take actions carrying a higher risk of war. Another concerned the potential impact of SALT on NATO with some Western Europeans feeling that the United States might give priority to the maintenace of good relations with the Soviet Union and that, in the process, she might be prepared to accept some erosion of Alliance solidarity and cohesion. And a third related to the possibility that future limitations on strategic armaments might affect Western European security either directly, *by hindering the modernisation and growth of independent nuclear forces* [author's italics], or indirectly, by reducing or redeploying American forces and weapons systems deemed essential to the maintenance of a military balance in Europe.[36]

Part of deterrence is the ability to defend if deterrence fails. The beauty, if that is the right word, of the original deterrent doctrine of immediate massive nuclear response was that it was simple and clear cut. It originated in the days of total US nuclear superiority and, as the Russians had no similar strategic response was, presumably, credible not only to the Western Allies but also to the Russians. Deterrence must be credible not only to those to be deterred but to those who intend to deter. It is this factor which has over the years, seen a development in NATO's deterrent policy. Once the Russians began to deploy their own nuclear systems then the question began to be asked 'would the US risk a nuclear retaliation on themselves if there was a conventional incursion into Western Europe?'

'Doubts about the threat of strategic nuclear retaliation as a deterrent to conventional aggression led to NATO's "flexible response" strategy in the sixties, calling for a spectrum of deterrence based on sound conventional defence.'[37] It was in the 1960s therefore that the role of non-nuclear forces began to assume a more significant place within the whole nuclear deterrent strategy. Unfortunately the consequences which should have inevitably flowed from such a change in deterrent posture were ignored by political leaders in Europe in general and in the UK in particular. If conventional forces are to assume a significant role in deterrence, this role can only be in an increased capability of fighting an actual war. In other words a credible conventional deterrence relies not in the fear of retaliation but as an observable capability on the part of the 'defenders' to successfully hold, at the very least, the land forces of the 'attacker'. Unfortunately, as far as the UK, is concerned, the 1957 White Paper had proposed the end of National Service and by the 1960s the British Armed Services were constituted on an all-Regular basis. So, at the very time that NATO's deterrence policy, if it was to be credible, would require large conventional forces backed up by trained reserve manpower, the UK began the process of reducing her forces and ensuring that in time, she would cease to have a pool of reserve manpower which had had some form of training, the ex-National Servicemen.

FLEXIBLE RESPONSE

Once flexible response became the generally accepted NATO doctrine there was an immediate effect on the General Defence Plans in all the NATO regions, but none more so than in the Central Region. Up till then the practical problems faced by the land forces' commander were confined, more or less, to getting the divisions as quickly as possible to their initial fighting locations, particularly if there was very little or no warning of the attack; after initial contact their next task would be, by holding ground, to force the attackers to concentrate their formation to 'fight through' the defence. In the meantime the nuclear retaliation would have been unleashed and, hopefully, the fighting on the ground would stop in a fairly short time.

However once NATO's use of nuclear weapons ceased to be automatic her land forces were going to have to be prepared to fight for an unspecified number of days at a conventional level only. Here numbers become important. But numbers are not the only measure of conventional forces as there are many imponderables which will affect the actual battle – state of training, morale, the type of units, luck, and so on. This is not the chapter to enter into these problems and possible solutions to deterring and fighting a limited, in the initial stages, war in Europe except in so far as it affects the nuclear question. But West Germany began to see fairly quickly that a strategy which allowed a number of days' conventional fighting meant that she was going to be both the conventional and nuclear battleground. Hence the forward defence strategy was introduced.

This pressure resulted in the NATO ministers giving detailed political, strategic and economic guidance to the NATO military authorities. In December 1967 the Military Committee Concept (MC 14/3) which had been prepared in accordance with previous ministerial guidance was approved: the Communiqué of the Ministerial Meeting of the North Atlantic Council, held at the Brussels HQ on 13/14 December 1967, para. 12, reads as follows:

> This concept, which adapts NATO's strategy to current political, military and technological developments, is based upon a flexible and balanced range of appropriate responses, conventional and nuclear, to all levels of aggression or threats of aggression. These responses, subject to appropriate political control, are designed, first, to deter aggression and thus to preserve peace; but, should aggression unhappily occur, to maintain the security and integrity of the North Atlantic Treaty *within the concept of forward defence*. [author's emphasis]

Forward defence

The consequences of a forward defence are obvious and inevitable. However, yet again the politicans have either ignored or refused to believe what needs to be done to make a conventional forward defence a credible posture, not only to the Russians but to their own soldiers. There is no point ultimately in producing a defensive posture which is built upon a fraud. If a forward defence is going to be effective, it needs more Divisions than a 'delaying' defence where the defenders withdraw before being overrun. If the numbers are not increased, then the time that the defence can hold out will be shortened. This in turn means that recourse to nuclear weapons will have to be earlier. Thus the 'flexible response' allied to a 'forward defence' without a significant increase in the defending armies leads to an inflexible choice – early use of nuclear weapons or defeat. We shall return to this problem later. But if flexible reponse is to be a reality it needs some form of nuclear weaponry to back it up. The questions to be asked are:

What kind of nuclear weapons?
What delivery means?
How many, and of what yield, are needed?
Who will have control of these weapons?

It is in this area of short/medium range 'tactical' nuclear weapons that we, and NATO, are faced with looking hard at what happens if deterrence fails. The introduction of land based, Army manned, tactical nuclear weapons at present the Lance system (a rocket with a range of up to 110 km) and shells (fired from 208 mm and 155 mm guns with ranges up to 21 km) has given military commanders the capability of inflicting enormous damage upon opposing forces (after nuclear release, a political decision). However, does the possession of these systems actually contribute either to deterrence or to the war-fighting capability of NATO land forces if it has failed?

It is said, and put over at military training establishments that tactical nuclear weapons can redress the imbalance of numbers. For the sake of the argument this line will be followed within the context of the Central Region. All the NATO Corps are supported by Missile regiments equipped with Lance and/or nuclear (gun) artillery. However, they will only be used in anger if deterrence has failed and NATO is faced with a conventional or nuclear supported major attack in West Germany. They are not retaliatory but fighting weapons. The theory behind their use is that by the use of natural features (woods, hills, rivers), minefields and held positions, the aggressor forces if they are to continue to advance will be forced to concentrate, thus presenting worthwhile tactical nuclear targets. This is all good stuff. However, if the aggressor also has tactical nuclear weapons and it becomes a matter of attrition, the large army will beat the small one. So it might well be that tactical nuclear weapons, if by being used provoke a response in kind, could place the NATO forces in an even worse position than they were before.

The problem of security

Another problem is that of the security of these weapons before their use. Not only are units required to deploy the systems but others are needed to guard them. So if, for instance, the British Corps has a manpower ceiling, the fact that part of it is diverted to guarding the deployment of nuclear regiments means that there is less of it to actually fight the pre-nuclear battle. Reserve units that might well have a useful role elsewhere are having to guard these weapons which may never be used. But paradoxically it could be because of the absence of these very units which ensures that the request for 'release' has to be made early rather than late.

The guns of course could be used as ordinary artillery before nuclear release. Even here theory is not likely to work in practice. The deployment and use of medium artillery in the conventional role is different from the nuclear role. Guns in action can be spotted and attacked. Tactical nuclear artillery would remain silent and hidden until needed. Then, if used in anger, it would do so on a 'shoot and scoot' system. This entails moving quickly into a pre-surveyed gun position just before H hour (the time that the strike has been ordered) – firing the round and immediately moving. The artillery commander who uses his nuclear capable artillery to support the hard pressed tank and infantry units in the pre-nuclear phases runs the risk of losing some, or at worst all, of his potential nuclear delivery means. On the other hand, the more conventional artillery the better, and longer, will be the defence. In this respect the problem facing artillery commanders is similar to that facing the air force commanders.

Throughout this conventional phase one of the aims of the aggressor commanders at all levels will be to find and destroy, or capture, the NATO short range nuclear systems. The loss of any of these systems will represent a loss of potential fire-power in excess of all the conventional artillery deployed in the Central Region. This itself could be a destabilising factor in the minds of the NATO commanders. For not only might a decision on nuclear release have to be made because the defence cannot hold, but also because, if too many of NATO's nuclear units have been eliminated, the capability to use the weapons at all will be in danger of being lost. It would seem therefore that short range guns and rockets are not the best delivery systems for a forward defence posture and that for good sensible tactical reasons these systems should be removed and their tactical role taken on by aircraft from the Allied Tactical Air Forces or by allocating some Cruise missiles, which with their long range and accuracy should be able to perform the function whilst remaining relatively invulnerable to attack.

In any event talk of being able to conduct sensible military operations on land with nuclear weapons is mad. There will not be a limited nuclear war on land. Escalation will be swift. But, by having short range relatively low yield weapons, NATO might be giving the impression that a limited nuclear war on Continental Europe is a conceivable and planned for option. Deterrence will be better served if all the artillery available is conventional. Thus, by releasing missile and guarding units, the numbers of fighting units in position and the weight of supporting fire power to NATO's ground force commanders will be increased. In the meantime NATO's nuclear deterrent capability will still remain and be seen to remain.

CONVENTIONAL FORCES AND DETERRENCE

There are powerful voices which suggest that the flexible response strategy should be taken one stage further which is for NATO to develop a conventional deterrent strategy. This would be linked presumably with a declaration, by NATO, of 'no first use' of nuclear weapons. Although a non-nuclear argument it can only be considered in the context of NATO's overall deterrent strategy and is clearly an intellectual approach which must be addressed.

In the meantime received wisdom in NATO appears to be that a limited nuclear war is not possible. This is probably so on land, where, if either side strikes, there are going to be an enormous number of non-military casualties. Vengeance could be a factor in the retaliatory strikes, and once started 'any nuclear escalation would enter a vast unknown with unlimited possibilities for Murphy's law and panic and miscalculation'.[38]

However what about at sea? Fleets operate in the vast unpopulated oceans; they are manned in the main by regular professional sailors. A naval battle however horrendous would not have the same impact as a savage battle fought in, say, Hanover and its surrounds. Could it be that it is just conceivable that the nuclear powers might be able to accept tactical nuclear weapons used against them at sea and that their response would also be limited geographically to the sea?[39] A successful strike by a torpedo armed with a small tactical nuclear warhead could be responded to by an equally small nuclear depth charge. Such a conflict might not be easily contained at sea for long but that such a concept is well within the NATO 'flexible response' doctrine. The UK and NATO, should look very seriously at this. To present the more perfect deterrent the Royal Navy must be capable of fighting such a war, thus contributing to deterrence overall. So much for the questions; the answers are far more difficult.

8 A Nuclear Answer?

Being an independent middle ranking nuclear power is an expensive business. As nuclear weapons really only make sense in their deterrent role, those powers other than the USA and the USSR who opt to join, and having joined to remain in, the 'nuclear club', must be certain that the very considerable costs involved are in fact worthwhile. To be cost effective the deterrent must therefore be real.

It was, and this should never be forgotten, a Labour Government which took the original decision to make Britain an independent nuclear power. The strategic deterrent was in the hands of the Royal Air Force and consisted of bombs carried by the Victor and Vulcan fleets. Although small, the force was nevertheless extremely professional and was constantly able to demonstrate its effectiveness by means of dispersal exercises, immediate readiness drills and so on. Those aircrew that took part in the American Strategic Air Command bombing competitions always did well and no doubt contributed to the general level of confidence that the United States had in its closest European ally.

FROM INDEPENDENCE TO DEPENDENCE

What is not generally realised is that it was during the Conservative administrations, during some thirteen consecutive years of power, that Britain moved from being a totally independent nuclear power to one with a dependent nuclear force under national control.

The year 1956 can be taken as being when the thrust of Britain's policy ensured that she would, at some point, cease to have a totally independent nuclear deterrent force. Out of the political débâcle commonly called the Suez Crisis, Britain and France both drew totally opposite conclusions. France decided that she should never allow herself to be reliant on the United States where her own (France's) perceived vital interests were at stake. Not to put too fine a point on it, France would never trust the US again. Britain on the other hand, under Macmillan, who became Prime Minister in place of the ailing Anthony Eden, decided that her future must lie in the closest co-operation with the United States. This was not a matter of sentimentality or the fostering of an Anglo-Saxon special relationship, but based on the firm belief that the ultimate security of Britain, and indeed the rest of Western Europe, depended upon a vibrant, live and healthy Atlantic alliance. Possibly the greatest achievement of Harold Macmillan's premiership was the binding together, particularly after the Suez trauma, of the USA and UK.

However, one of the consequences of this relationship was the demise of Britain's independence as a nuclear power. This was not the fault of the USA. Blame has to be put fair and square on the shoulders of the Conservative administration of Macmillan. It is quite possible that the British government did not, during the mid and late 1950s, actually believe that a wholly independent national nuclear force, in the sense that quite clearly France did, was a necessity or even particularly desirable. In a 'Declaration of Common Purpose' made by President Eisenhower and Prime Minister Macmillan on 25 October 1957 the following statement was included:

> The concept of national self-sufficiency is now out of date. The countries of the free world are now interdependent, and only in genuine partnership, by combining the resources and sharing many tasks in many fields, can progress and safety be found.[40]

This concept of interdependence could of course be applied not only to conventional defence forces, and foreign policies, but also to nuclear forces at all levels of deterrence.

The 1957 Defence White Paper quite firmly placed the emphasis on security through nuclear deterrence. The strategic concept underlying this deterrence was the immediate and massive nuclear response to any Soviet aggression. Unfortunately such a strategy is relatively cheap, as the level of conventional forces does not have to be particularly high. The problem today is that reliance on nuclear weapons, in the event of deterrence failing, is almost total. Yet this reliance has itself become less and less credible. Indeed, there is a case to be made that European and British politicians in power have deliberately maintained a nuclear posture, knowing that the strategy itself was incredible to themselves, but also knowing that any credible alternative would be more expensive. The chickens are now coming home to roost for all the NATO European powers including Great Britain.

The closeness with which the United States and the United Kingdom have worked in the nuclear field over the years can be seen in the number of US delivery systems that have been stationed in the UK. In

1958, for instance, 60 Thor 1 RBMs began to be deployed in Britain. These were under joint US–UK control and were manned by RAF personnel.[41] Subsequently a number of British bases were made available for some of the USAF fighter-bombers which the French no longer wished to be deployed on French soil.

Meanwhile Britain's own nuclear programme continued apace. But strategic political decisions which were at the time clearly wrong were being taken by the British (Conservative) government. The successor to the V-bomber force was to be Blue Streak, which would begin to replace the manned bombers in the mid-1960s. Blue Streak, however, was a liquid-fuelled rocket system with a range of about 2000 miles and would be deployed in, and fired from, unhardened silos. It was therefore from its inception already obsolete. The measure of its strategic uselessness was underlined by its own operational limitations. The completed Fylingdales radar station as part of the US (NATO) Early Warning (EW) system would give Britain four minutes warning time. Blue Streak took some 20 minutes to fuel up. It could therefore only be a first strike weapon. The essential requirement of any first strike system is that the launch of such a pre-emptive attack would ensure the destruction of virtually all of the opponent's nuclear striking capability. Britain's nuclear force would never be large enough to do this. Thus quite obviously, as it would not be able to perform that function, it would never be a credible deterrent system. What Britain's need then in the context of nuclear deterrence, was a second strike capacity of a certain minimum capability. It was therefore clear at a very early stage that Blue Streak could never be a realistic replacement for the V-bomber force. Yet the British Government of the day refused to take the decision to cancel the project. Eventually in 1960 the decision to cancel was taken. The sheer waste of financial, technical, management and capital resources involved because of the failure to take the inevitable decision at an early stage were horrendous. It was now that the Conservative Government took the decision which was to ensure that independence in the nuclear game was to become a *de facto* dependence.

SKYBOLT

An agreement was reached with the Americans that Skybolt, a stand-off air launched ballistic missile, would be on offer. The attractions to the British government of the day were several. First, Britain would remain in the nuclear club – this was politically necessary to quieten the Conservative backbenchers who would otherwise have been uncontrollably depressed at the cancellation of Blue Streak, secondly the life of the V-bomber would be extended and, thirdly cheapness. *The Guardian* at the time raised the doubts over the Skybolt arrangement:

> One cannot call oneself independent if the wherewithal for independence is supplied by someone else. If Britain is to depend on the US for supplies of modern nuclear weapons she will not be an independent nuclear power – and no amount of rhetoric will convince anyone outside the backbenchers of the Conservative Party that she is.[42]

Watkinson, one of a line of singularly undistinguished Conservative Defence Ministers who came and went at the remarkable rate of about one a year, defended the agreement and stated in the House of Commons on 22 April 1960:

> If the weapon is developed and we purchase it without strings, fit it with our own warhead, and carry it in our own aircraft, then it is an independent deterrent.

By the time Thorneycroft had become Minister of Defence in 1962, Skybolt was cancelled by the Americans. So much for independence.

The political uproar that the cancellation of Skybolt could have caused was probably underestimated by the Americans, to whom the decision was almost certainly a technical one – the system did not work, so cancel it. It is likely that McNamara, the US Secretary of State for Defence, secretly hoped that this would be the end of Britain's independent nuclear role. He had already expressed his doubts on the desirability of small independently controlled nuclear forces:

> Limited nuclear capabilities, operating independently, are dangerous, expensive, prone to obsolescence and lacking in credibility as a deterrent.[43]

President Kennedy had also publicly depreciated the utility of independent nuclear forces.[44] However, it was not too fanciful to suggest that the political future of the Conservative Government depended upon a form of solution which maintained the appearance of a Great Britain still in the nuclear club. Strategic thought went out of the window for 'what was at stake was a fiction on which Britain's postwar policy had been based and for which successive British governments expended 10 billion dollars'.[45]

Conservative governments have always tried to get defence on the cheap. The chance of getting a nuclear weapon system at cost or nearly so, Skybolt, was too much of a temptation. No matter that it had not been bought by the Americans which was not surprising, since, even after the expenditure of 2½ billion dollars, the missile had still not been successfully tested.[50] Thus, as a result of a series of bad decisions, lack of courage and parsimony, Britain, unlike France, ceased to be a truly independent nuclear power.

POLARIS

The eventual result, for good or ill, was the Nassau Agreement, by which, in an ambiguously worded document, Britain retained a nationally controlled strategic nuclear force, based on the Polaris system. The Royal Navy was to take on the task of operating the British nuclear deterrent force. It is certain that, as the political survival of the Government was at stake, little thought had been given to the impact that the Nassau Agreement would have on either Britain's future relations with Europe, in particular France, on the one hand, and the inevitable implications that it would also have for Britain's defence policy and the future structure of the Royal Navy on the other. Polaris, once operational, did at least give Britain a credible second strike capability, the essence of a nuclear deterrent strategy. However, the reduction in actual destructive capability between the Polaris force of four boats with 16 missiles each and full V-bomber force was considerable. Indeed, to have retained the equivalent destructive power of the old V-bomber force, Britain would have needed 20 Polaris submarines. It must be debatable therefore, despite the power represented by the four Polaris boats, which in effect means one or possibly two on station at any one time, that in fact Britain at present has an 'independent' deterrent that is neither independent nor a deterrent.

It would be wrong to underestimate the power represented by a Polaris on station, however. Together with the French *force de frappe*, the fact is that European NATO does possess nuclear deterrent power of some significance. Whether formally allocated to NATO with targeting done by NATO as the British force is, or purely national in the case of the French system, it does mean that there are, ultimately, two centres of decision taking, apart from the President of the United States, within NATO. This would be a factor if the time ever came that the Soviet Union was to approach the point at which she was seriously considering using military means to change the political balance in Europe. The problem is where should we go from here? The present answer is that the existing situation of dependence upon the USA should continue and that Polaris, which will remain operational with certain improvements to the system, until the early to mid-1990s, will be replaced by Trident.

TRIDENT

Trident has all the advantages of Polaris, only more so. It will still be a significant second strike retaliatory weapon system. The destructive power of the total inventory is many times that of Polaris and in a situation where hopefully nuclear reduction talks will be continuing between East and West this might be unfortunate. One thing therefore that should be done is for a study to be carried out to see what the minimum force would be required to provide an effective deterrent. If the power represented by the UK Polaris force is considered to be sufficient not only within the context of NATO but also, apparently, in the situation where the system might have to deter outside NATO, there seems little point in increasing this level of power. If, on the other hand, the new level of power which Trident will provide is considered correct, presumably the present deterrence represented by the UK Polaris force is a myth. It could of course be that, coincidentally with the introduction of Trident, the minimum level of power needs to be increased.

If the Government persists with the Trident option it will not only perpetuate the distortion effect that Polaris has, and is having, on Britain's defence effort, it will, because of the relatively higher costs, make the situation worse. The shape of the Royal Navy has, despite repeated denials, been seriously affected by the existence of Polaris. If NATO is to get away from the strategic nuclear straitjacket that she has got herself into – the situation where effective non-nuclear defence has been sacrificed for a nuclear deterrent posture – something must be done. Politically it is not desirable that the difference in relationship between the United States and Britain and France in nuclear matters should continue. Britian really ought to take the opportunity, which the phasing out of Polaris offers, to initiate closer co-operation with France. Each country is faced with the same basic problem, the cost of maintaining nuclear forces separate from those of the United States. The time surely has come where the two Western European NATO nuclear powers must begin to cooperate if their deterrent forces are to continue to represent a believable form of non-US, NATO, nuclear military power.

THE BRITISH/FRENCH SITUATION

It would be a mistake to ascribe France's 'go it alone' policy in both the nuclear and non-nuclear fields to de Gaulle alone. His view of France's role whilst he was in power was essentially that of the vast majority of the French people. However, even the most ardently nationalistic Frenchman must be aware of the enormous costs, in comparative terms, for a non-superpower to maintain a credible independently developed and controlled nuclear deterrent force. Close co-operation in the continuing development of the British and French nuclear forces should not be regarded as being anti-American but rather pro-European. Integration of the French and British nuclear forces should not be the aim. Even if possible, such a policy aim would, certainly in the medium and short term, be unacceptable to the French. If thought to be an eventual long term British objective, this would be sufficient, probably, to ensure that any form of co-operation would be, from the French point of view, a non-starter. The aims therefore of British/French nuclear policies should be the rationalisation of research and development which would certainly cut costs, the spreading of the design and production effort, and, finally, the creation, by the mid to late 1990s, of two nationally controlled and built nuclear forces which are complementary to one another with command, control and planning arrangements which allow for the closest possible cooperation, short of integrated command.

Before proceeding with any policy on these lines the government must carry the electorate with it in the belief that a British nuclear deterrent force under national command is not only desirable but necessary. The argument at present advanced appears to be that, ultimately, Britain needs her own deterrent in the event that her own vital national interests are at stake. Just where, outside the NATO context, Britain's interests will clash with the Soviet Union's no one appears to know. Yet in referring to the Trident system in the statement on the Defence Estimates 1981, there is a most interesting sentence: 'Like Polaris it (Trident) will be committed to NATO *save in a situation where our supreme national interests are at stake*'[47] [author's emphasis].

The argument or hint that somehow the UK will actually face the USSR alone outside NATO in a situation where 'supreme national interests are at stake' seems quite extraordinary. It is indeed a piece of sophistry which weakens the already perfectly good case for a European based, owned and commanded nuclear deterrent force.

THE NEED FOR A EUROPEAN NUCLEAR CONTRIBUTION

For too long the balance of power in NATO has been unhealthily, in political terms, in favour of the Americans. This has meant that not only has she spent more than she need have done if she had followed an isolationist course after 1945, but the burden of ultimate responsibility for the viability of the alliance has been too one-sided. To be frank, the European powers have been able, because of the US nuclear umbrella, to have defence on the cheap.

This must now stop for two reasons: firstly, Europe can never be truly considered either by herself or others to be the free, self-confident society that her economic position entitles her to be and, secondly, unless the Europeans are seen by the Americans to be taking a fairer share of the overall defence of NATO, those voices in the United States urging some form of pull out from Europe will be listened to with increasing attention and sympathy. The other argument is that a second (or, counting France, a third) nuclear decision-making authority in NATO which is European based must increase the whole deterrent posture of NATO in Soviet eyes. As the statement on the Defence Estimates put it in 1981:

> Even if in some future situation Soviet leaders imagined that the United States might not be prepared to use nuclear weapons, having to take account of enormous destructive power in European hands would compel them to regard the risks of aggression in Europe as still very grave. This additional element of insurance – the 'second centre of decision' – has been a feature of alliance deterrence for over twenty-five years.[48]

However, what is inconceivable is a situation outside the NATO context in which the UK might actually have to rely upon its own nationally controlled nuclear deterrent forces against any other power. If this is so, then this should effect the type of nuclear force that the UK would need to fulfil the second centre of NATO decision-making function. This would increase the effectiveness of NATO's overall deterrence strategy.

What Britain (and France) require is the ability to start a nuclear war not to continue or end it. This is one aspect of nuclear deterrence. Talk of actually winning a limited nuclear war is meaningless. As part of deterrence strategy military planners have to look beyond the point at which deterrence fails. Plans exist to fight in the nuclear environment. Military training obviously has to be carried out so that doctrine can be developed for the conduct of operations in support of nuclear force. By being seen to be prepared to fight a nuclear war NATO conventional armed forces are themselves contributing to the overall deterrent posture. Nevertheless the military know that they are training, certainly in Central Europe, for the unthinkable. No one can tell what a tactical nuclear war would be like, fought as it would be in East and West Germany as well as possibly other countries.

TACTICAL NUCLEAR WEAPONS

This leads to the area of short range tactical nuclear weapons. They were originally introduced into the NATO inventory in the Central Region when NATO's belief was that a major non-nuclear WP aggression could only be halted by the use of tactical nuclear weapons.

NATO's nuclear forces must have two tasks if deterrence fails – the first, to be able to influence the local tactical situation and the second, to inflict sufficient punishment on an aggressor so that he is forced to the negotiating table. The second is likely to require the use of strategic nuclear weapons and could of course succeed without immediately affecting the first. This really is one reason for having nuclear weapons at more than one level of deterrence. A weakness or absence of a weapons system at any level of fighting capability is significant, not so much in the reduced nuclear fighting potential, but, because of this reduction, the whole deterrence posture is weakened. The aim of nuclear weapons is to deter, not to defeat an enemy in war because deterrence has failed.

The problems facing the NATO corps commanders in the Central

Region with regard to the security of the short range tactical nuclear weapons under their operational control have already been discussed. The vulnerability of these weapons, because they have to be deployed so far forward, is itself a destablising factor. NATO cannot afford to lose these weapons, either by their discovery and destruction, and all that has to be put out of action is the delivery means, by air or ground attack or their capture, an even worse thought; nor can the WP afford to have its own short and medium range ground launched nuclear weapons destroyed by the NATO ATAFs.

The time has come, if a forward defence flexible response strategy is to make more sense at corps level and below, to remove this class of weapon from the battlefield altogether. The critical factor with tactical nuclear weapons is not the range of the delivery means, be it rocket or gun, but the yield of the warhead and the level of assurance that ground zero (GZ) – the point on the ground below the burst – is close to the target. The introduction of Cruise nuclear missiles into Europe gives NATO the chance of using this system to replace the short range systems. Cruise is extremely accurate and has sufficient range to allow its deployment well to the rear (westwards) of the forward battle area. Indeed there seems no reason, other than communications, why Cruise missiles based in the UK could not be used to strike at targets in support of the four NORTHAG army corps. The system is extremely accurate and the response time could be sufficiently fast, bearing in mind the many drills and procedures that have to be gone through before a nuclear weapon is fired, for this to be a perfectly reasonable alternative means of delivery. Of course the command, control and communications arrangements would have to be developed but certainly the technical requirements to ensure a high degree of certainty of response could be met.

Before initial nuclear release is given, no one below the decision taker, the President of the United States personally or, in the case of Britain's and France's own national forces, the Prime Minister, or President can authorise the use of any nuclear weapon of any level. No army commander at any level likes having forces under his command or control that he cannot use to influence the battle. He is in the normal course of events given a task and certain resources and expected to get on with it. The putting of strings on some of his elements of power is to remove his tactical power of command. So it is with short range nuclear weapons. They are of no use in the non-nuclear battle, yet every commander who has them is responsible for them. No commander likes responsibility without power.

THE REMOVAL OF LAND SHORT RANGE TACTICAL NUCLEAR WEAPONS

Thus the concept of tactical nuclear weapon delivery systems being either aircraft or Cruise missiles can remove entirely from corps and divisional commanders the responsibility for their security is one which seems to offer the best solution to this problem. The resources at present tied up in guarding and deploying the existing short range systems can then be used in the more profitable roles of actively contributing to the non-nuclear tactical battle. This would certainly be a more rational situation so long as the communications which will have to be set up will ensure the same, or nearly so, speed of response, once nuclear release has been authorised. This, in fact, would not be a problem.

Such a removal of one level of nuclear weapons by NATO, the short range land based rockets and in the case of the guns their nuclear shells, will not reduce the nuclear fighting potential of the forward army corps. It will, however, make the negotiation of a belt of territory between East and West to be 'out of bounds' to the peace-time deployment of nuclear weapons rather easier. It is important that, without in any way putting NATO at a tactical disadvantage, the other aim of the West's nuclear deterrence policy is pursued with as much vigour as the deployment plans. That is the reduction of the level of nuclear weapons on both sides. If therefore certain unilateral moves can be made which would allow the Soviets to follow suit, then the process of developing confidence building measures can begin. This particular area, the short range land based nuclear weapons is a realistic starting point, now that Cruise has been deployed.

NATO could in fact remove all this class of weapon now without in any way reducing its fighting potential. 2 and 4 ATAFs could take on part of the role of supporting the forward Corps with small yield tactical nuclear weapons. Probably it would take up to twelve months for the command, control and communications arrangements to be set up, so that a number of Cruise missile units can be assigned to SACEUR for the support of the eight Army corps in the Central Region.

In the tactical nuclear area a considerable amount of contingency planning has been developed. All corps commanders have a good idea as to where and in what circumstances nuclear release might be given. Indeed the WINTEX series of exercises produce an interesting consistency in the pattern of decision making. Thus there is little doubt that a large number of contingency programmes can be fed into the computer systems of Cruise on the basis of anticipated target locations. The military is well aware that the best laid plans seldom survive contact. Nevertheless as part of NATO's deterrent strategy there would be little doubt in Soviet minds that if it came to the point, NATO could still use tactical nuclear weapons.

THE UK's NUCLEAR POSTURE

What then of Great Britain's nuclear posture? In national terms do the present plans of the government make sense? Accepting that Britain is to remain a nuclear power and not, as all the other European NATO states, with the exception of France, a non-nuclear power within a nuclear alliance, are the resources in money, material, and skilled manpower going to be best used in maintaining a nuclear deterrent of last resort? To think that Britain's independent deterrent will ever have a role outside the NATO context is unbelievable. The only realistic view is to accept that both France and Britain's deterrent forces are part of the overall NATO deterrent, even though, in terms of destructive power, a small part. As a part of a larger whole they both have significance, alone they have an unquantifiable amount. Unless both the French and British governments face this fact neither is likely to produce the most sensible and cost effective nationally commanded nuclear forces. So, within NATO, what should be the shape of Britain's deterrent force?

NATO has moved from the virtually automatic nuclear response to a more flexible approach. Hence, within the inventory, there are different types of weapons systems appropriate to various levels of deterrence. Although, if any nuclear weapon is used in anger, deterrence will have failed, it is possible to postulate that, even after the initial strike, an element of deterrence still remains. Although it is generally accepted that there will be no such thing as a limited nuclear war in the Central Region, planning has to proceed on the basis that escalation from one level of nuclear use to the next is not necessarily going to be automatic. The initial use of a tactical low yield weapon would have two aims – the first, to influence the local military situation immediately, and the second to give a clear signal to the aggressor that NATO is indeed prepared to escalate. Therefore, in a sense, the initial use of a nuclear weapon by NATO – and let us remember that NATO will not initiate hostilities – would still have a deterrent element, despite deterrence having failed.

The basic reason, underlying all others including the verbiage generated in the nuclear debate, why Western Europe needs some form of nuclear deterrent forces not under American control, is the fear that the United States might not be prepared to go nuclear in circumstances in which European interests require such escalation. Even if the United States would, in the event, have been prepared to use her nuclear weapons, if the Soviets should ever doubt this, then deterrence is weakened. Although not explicitly spelt out in the 1981 White Paper this must surely be the reasoning behind the reference to the 'second centre of decision'. The requirement for the UK then is not to have nuclear forces that can, of themselves, inflict unacceptable damage upon an aggressor, but to have sufficient nuclear forces to initiate the quantum jump from non-nuclear operations to nuclear war. Once this truth has been grasped then the type of nuclear delivery systems needed by Britain can be reassessed. What actually is needed is not an independent nuclear deterrent of 'last resort' which is the present policy, but a deterrent force of 'initial use' which has sufficient diversification of delivery means to retain a high probablity of a 'second strike' capability. As the 1981 White Paper points out the choice of delivery vehicle lies between Cruise and ballistic missiles.[49] Now, although this remark was made in the context of justifying the choice of Trident, if the *raison d'être* of the British nuclear deterrent ceases to have any function outside the NATO context, then the level of deterrence represented by the Trident solution is the wrong one for the UK.

All NATO and UK defence planning is done on the assumption that the West will not initiate military operations against the Soviet Union or Warsaw Pact unless in response to aggression. Whatever scenario one paints, can there be any conceivable circumstances when the UK by itself would launch a strategic nuclear strike against the USSR? This is what the Trident solution implies could happen. Surely if the flexible response is to be developed over the next twenty years or so, and the alternative to flexible response is immediate nuclear response, then the UK nuclear force, if it is to reflect this flexibility of response, must enable Britain to be able to be seen to have the capability of initiating the first stages of nuclear war and not the final act. This can be done with a nuclear force based on a mix of Cruise systems, both surface and air launched. There is a strong case that at least half the surface launched missiles should be shipborne. In this respect Cruise missiles should also be deployed on submarines and possibly a fleet of small ships (hydrofoils and hovercraft?) to ensure that a 'first strike' option against the UK nuclear force would not achieve its aim.

Such a force can have a dual role, that is to say the ships, aircraft and ground units, would have non-nuclear tactical capabilities as well. The costs of maintaining the national nuclear deterrent, which at present do not contribute in any way to the conventional capabilities of the overall defence effort, would now be part of the non-nuclear effort. This argument may appear to fly in the face of the conclusions concerning the land based short range nuclear weapons at present deployed in Germany. The essential difference, however, is that the Cruise missile is a long range weapon. Its accuracy is not degraded by lengthening its range. Security against surprise attack is not the problem that it is with the present Lance missiles in Germany.

The possibility of a limited nuclear war at sea has been touched upon. In order to strengthen NATO's posture in the Northern Region, the alliance should develop the capacity of being able to conduct such limited nuclear operations against the Northern Fleet, as part of the general NATO deterrence. The UK is uniquely placed to take on this role.

The Trident programme should be cancelled now. The maximum return should be obtained out of the existing Polaris system and its operational effectiveness should certainly be extended into the mid-1990s. This allows Britain some ten years to introduce her 'post-Polaris' nuclear force. In order to preserve maximum tactical flexibility of the system total reliance on computer controlled rockets is unwise. Manned aircraft will still have a role to play in a nuclear deterrent force at the level of deterrence that the UK needs. The dual role capability of Cruise should be developed, so that there are some units equipped with missiles with non-nuclear warheads.

As the first part of the programme the British government should now enter into negotiations with the Americans to develop the next generation of Cruise. The French should also be approached in order that the two European NATO nuclear forces may be developed as complementary systems.

In the meantime, there is a strong case for the existing Cruise missile units to be dual manned. The RAF Regiment should be expanded so that it can take on this role. Initially RAF personnel, which have a considerable security role in any case, could be introduced into the US units to take on some of the 'nuts and bolts' tasks such as driving, etc. Then, over a period of time, complete missile detachments would be

RAF manned so that by, say, 1990 all the UK based Cruise missile systems would be manned by the RAF. There seems no reason in fact why precisely the same dual control system, whereby the US warheads are kept under American custody until actual firing, which has for years worked perfectly well with the army short range rocket units in Germany, should not be introduced. Not only does it make good tactical sense but it would make extremely good political sense, as the visible dual control thus created would allay many of the doubts that have been raised in the minds of a significant number of British voters of all parties over the present situation, with regard to the alleged power of veto which the Prime Minister has with Cruise now.

The Royal Navy and Royal Air Force must still have their own tactical nuclear weapons. In the case of the Navy these may include mines, torpedoes and SS rockets and for the RAF a mix of bombs and Cruise-type delivery systems. The Army needs no delivery means of its own, as the change in our nuclear policy would proceed with the re-deployment plans that have been suggested. The actual delivery of nuclear strikes in support of land forces should be done by the ATAFs in the Central Region and by naval or air forces in the Northern Region.

9 The Defence of the Homeland

The basis of any defence policy must be the security of the homeland. In strategic terms it is desirable that the 'front line' should be projected outwards as far as possible. It is this which, in part, forms the basis of all post-war Governments' adherence to the Central Front strategy. The front line, it has been considered, is northern Germany.

This strategy makes sense for France, Holland and Belgium but does it still fit Great Britain? Unlike her European continental allies, Britain is an island separated from all her neighbours by the sea. To a unique extent therefore the UK is dependent upon imports, all of which essentially arrive by sea. Dependence on the security of the high seas and the waters around these islands has, if anything, increased over the past 40 years. This is despite the fact that British agriculture is one of the major industries of the country. North Sea oil has made Britain an overall ex-porter of fossil fuels. The security therefore of the British oil rigs and pipelines must be considered as much a part of the overall home defence requirement as is the defence of other vital points such as nuclear-powered, oil-fired and coal-fired power stations, airfields and bridges, etc.

In recent years a considerable amount has been done to improve the situation as far as home defence is concerned. However the question as to how much of our defence resources should be allocated to the prime task of defence at home as opposed to distant defence of the country, which is the present role of the British Army of the Rhine and Royal Air Force Germany, has not really been faced. This is fundamental. It is upon this answer that the whole basis of British defence strategy rests. Essentially the case against all British Governments since the Second World War is that they have allowed a momentum to build up over the years in favour of the so-called continental strategy. This has resulted not only in a lack of real independence in the strategic nuclear deterrent role for reasons that have been discussed in earlier chapters, and which, for instance, France still retains, but also in a dangerous imbalance in the deployment of land forces which has left the home base vulnerable, not only to an internal threat from a fifth column movement but also from the possibility of invasion itself.

There are three elements which need to be considered when it comes to home defence in conflicts short of general nuclear war. These are, first, defence against air attack, whether by attack aircraft, missiles or airborne assault; second, defence against the maritime threat, including attacks against shipping and seaborne assault against Great Britain's North Sea islands and North Sea Oil rigs. The third element is the security of UK territory including vital points, airfields, railways, communication centres, etc., from what can be called 'small group' attacks as well as the need for an observable capability to resist successfully a sizeable force landed by air and/or amphibious assault.

Beyond this, however, lies the threat of nuclear or chemical/biological attack. How realistic is any preparation against such attack? There are those who say that there is no defence against nuclear attack and that any preparations in this respect are a farce and calculated to deceive. This is, in essence, part of the CND case against civil defence measures. What this movement never seems to consider is the possibility of a war in Europe which is not nuclear. In view of the known offensive chemical capability of the Russian Empire there seems every reason, if deterrence should ever fail, to suppose that the UK could well be subjected to a major strategic chemical attack rather than nuclear strikes.

In this respect it has to be said that the preparations in 1939 against gas attack (every civilian and serviceman had a personal gas mask) were far in advance of those in the mid-1980s. At present, in practical terms, although the armed forces are well prepared for chemical warfare (British defensive equipment is arguably the best in NATO), the civilian population is entirely defenceless, and indeed largely ignorant, as to the nature of the threat. This ignorance is partly due to the concentration by movements such as the CND on the horrors of nuclear war to the apparent exclusion of other types of conflict.

This matter of civil defence is important. By its very nature a civil defence organisation would not normally be activated unless deterrence has failed, or is seen to be about to fail. To that extent therefore money spent on this form of defence has a less visible return than that spent, for instance, on mobile forces which, as in the Falklands campaign, may well be used in conflicts short of general war.

THE CASE FOR A CIVIL DEFENCE

There are two points to consider, however, which do strengthen the case for a realistic civil defence organisation. The first is that an observably efficient civil defence might show to a potential aggressor that a country is actually prepared to defend itself (the examples of neutral Sweden and Switzerland are instructive in this respect). This preparedness would tend to add to the overall deterrent strategy of the country concerned. This is, if the basic aim is first and foremost to deter, surely desirable. Secondly, such an organisation can, indeed ought to, be used in non-military peace-time emergencies. It is of interest that in Britain this concept of emergency planning seems to have come initially from a number of councils, some of whom have voted themselves to be 'nuclear free'. Whatever the initiating motive, clearly a well organised and comprehensive emergency planning force which can be activated in the event of major disasters (Aberfan springs to mind) must be useful. This concept, welded together with that of 'planning for the worst case' would seem to be a means of uniting those who have grave doubts about the concept of civil defence and those who believe that some form of organised survival force is essential. The question then remains as to what kind of civil defence force the country should have and what capital and man-power resources should be allocated to it.

CIVIL DEFENCE ORGANISATION

Civil defence is the responsibility of the Home Office. Plans exist for the powers and responsibilities of Government, in the event of a major military attack on the UK, to be devolved to a number of regional headquarters. Senior ministers and officials have been ear-marked to these centres of political authority.[54] These measures though would only be put into effect if central government had lost the means to exercise effective control.

The basic structure of civil defence in England is as follows:

(a) 16 regions, each of which control
(b) 2 or 3 zones. These have under them
(c) counties, which control
(d) districts, below which are
(e) support areas with emergency advisers

To take one particular area of England, the West Midlands Region, the outline organisation consists of:

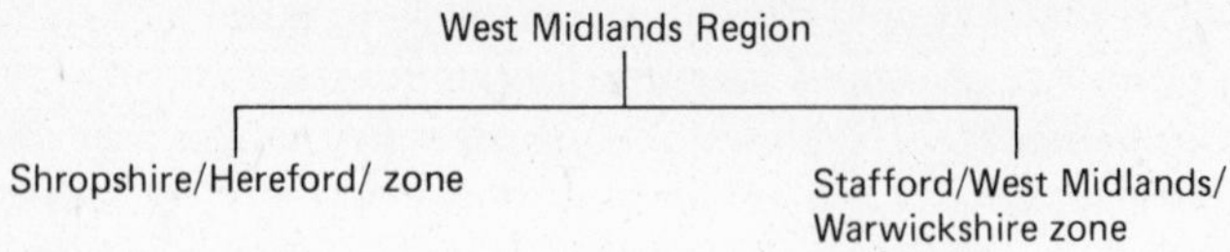

In the event of activation, the Regional Commissioner and his staff would deploy to the Shropshire/Hereford Zone HQ, whilst his deputy and staff would deploy to the Stafford/West Midlands/Warwick Zone HQ to create a stand-by regional HQ.

At county level there is, of course, a much greater degree of planning variety, not only because each county is different, with different problems, but because it is at this level, and below, that the present UK civil defence planning effort depends almost entirely upon unpaid voluntary effort. In Shropshire, for instance, peace-time planning is carried out by three full time emergency planning staff and six part-time staff. In fact, out of a total annual county budget of some £180 million only £110 000 is spent on emergency planning. An inhibiting factor which prevents planning becoming too detailed is the lack of formal powers in peace-time. Thus it is, in Shropshire, that the basic concept by which emergency planning is carried out is that, in the worst case, survival will depend upon the existence at the grass roots of a number of people who have some idea as to what must be done, and not much more.

Shropshire, the largest inland county in the UK, is largely rural and is located immediately west of the vast Midlands industrial conurbation of Birmingham and Wolverhampton. However, within its boundaries there are two sizeable urban concentrations, Telford and Shrewsbury. Its outline civil defence organisation consists of:

COUNTY

(a) *6 District Councils* each of which provides
(b) *a wartime emergency HQ*. Below these are a number of
(c) *support areas*, which contain
(d) *emergency advisers* who are all volunteers and unpaid.

It is here, depending upon the basic planning concept felt to be realistic, that either the essential weakness, or strength, of present civil defence planning in the UK is demonstrated.

Shropshire has been taken as an example as it does highlight some of the peace-time planning problems which face all emergency planners throughout the UK. It is interesting to note that the type of community appears to affect the number of volunteers prepared to act as emergency advisers. In Shropshire the 230 parishes are divided into 97 support areas. At the time of writing (mid-1985) there are approximately 450 registered emergency advisers throughout the county. What is significant is that it is in the rural areas that these volunteers are more easily found. Yet it could be said that it is in the urban areas where the need would, *in extremis*, be greater. It would seem, certainly in Shropshire, that the feeling of 'community' is significantly stronger in the country areas and in that sense a breakdown of order is less likely in the country parishes and villages than in the towns where the sense of 'belonging' is less strong.

WEAKNESSES IN THE PRESENT ORGANISATION

However, this level of argument is highly subjective. What is more serious is the political attitude towards civil defence. Of the six District Councils in Shropshire there are five which co-operate and one, Wrekin District Council, that does not. As a direct result of the attitude of the Wrekin District Council, there are no emergency planning advisers whatever within its area of responsibility. Yet, as an urban area, it is arguably one of the areas which really needs this basic infrastructure in peace-time.

This, there is no doubt, is the great and overriding weakness of civil defence planning in the UK. There are two possibilities. The first is to continue planning on a shoestring and in basic outline only (the present Shropshire concept), or to completely change the whole outlook towards civil defence by making it as much a part of the home defence of the UK as a whole, as, for instance, the air defence system is. This would require a fundamental change in outlook and concept.

THE CONCEPT OF TOTAL DEFENCE

This concept of the totality of defence is not new and the example of Norway is instructive. Norway, a NATO member, has no nuclear weapons of her own nor does she allow the permanent stationing of foreign troops on her soil in peace-time. However, as a NATO nation, she fully subscribes to the current NATO doctrine of non-aggressive deterrence based upon the possession, by the Alliance, of tactical and strategic nuclear forces.

Norway's example

Because her population is small, being only some 4 million, and her land area is large (in European NATO only France and Turkey are bigger) she needs, within her limited means, 'to utilize all [her] available resources, and to concentrate them into a maximum effort in the defence of the nation'.[51] Norway has therefore developed the concept of the totality of defence. Norway's defence problems are different from those of the UK and clearly her solutions are peculiar to her. Nevertheless some of the resultant concepts would have a relevance to the British situation.

The demarcation lines between military and civil responsibilities are drawn somewhat differently in Norway than most other NATO countries. A number of tasks which often belong to the military have been placed in the civil sector particularly in the logistic field.

This concept of 'total defence' has a number of advantages. The main one is that 'defence' ceases to be an area for professional experts but the basic concern of everybody. The feeling of a total commitment is very strong and it is one which should be encouraged in Britain. As General Bryntensen puts it in relation to his own country,

> The philosophy of Norway's total defence concept creates the *moral foundation* for our work, making it *an obligation for all*, civilian, political and administrative agencies, private organisations, firms and enterprises, to find and prepare for their role in a society thrown into a total effort to defend the country.[52] [Author's emphasis]

The seriousness and extent to which Norway has already taken her civil defence can be seen in the effort she has put (and is still putting) into the building of shelters. Private and public shelters have been built in Norway since 1948.

The aim is to provide up to 375 000 public shelter spaces and some 230 000 are now in existence with between seven and ten thousand a year still being built. Already, including the private shelters, there are facilities for over half the population, a remarkable achievement. Besides this, all industrial enterprises with more than 40 employees have their own civil defence organisations financed by each particular enterprise itself. As a result Norway has more than 30 000 people employed in civil defence units – that is to say one out of every 130 people is playing a positive role in peace-time in Norway's civil defence programme. If the UK was to consider taking civil defence as seriously, this could mean an active force of some 430 000 would come into existence.

A BRITISH RESPONSE

The social mores in Britain are, regretfully, such that neither firms nor individuals would voluntarily produce the effort needed to go anywhere near matching Norway's performance.

On the other hand if a need is shown to be there, and, also that the burden of filling that need is seen to be fair and equally shared, then the nation, if the past is anything to go by, would be prepared to go along with Government plans. What, therefore, we need is a realistic programme of education to convince the British that, firstly there is a threat, and, secondly that the threat can be contained by means short of war. However deterrence, for this is now what we are talking about, if it is to be realistic to a potential aggressor must be underpinned, as it is in Norway, by the visible manifestation of a national determination that, if deterrence should fail, the country is still nevertheless prepared to defend itself. Armed force has a part, indeed a vital part, to play in successful deterrence. What no recent British government has appeared to grasp is the equally important role that the people have to play.

To this end therefore civil defence ought to be considered as much a part of the overall defence of the country as is air defence or the deployment in the deterrent role of nuclear forces in peace-time. To achieve this, serious consideration needs to be given to civil defence becoming integrated into home defence and, as such, responsibility for peace-time planning, organisation and training should be taken over from the Home Office by the Ministry of Defence. There would be considerable planning difficulties to overcome but good liaison can still achieve effective cooperation between the military and civil defence forces and the police and other emergency aid agencies.

If large and effective civil defence units are to be raised, they will need training and the one organisation which has the necessary skills in sufficient quantity and the experience in the handling of large numbers of recruits is the army.

What, however, will be needed is numbers. Almost certainly after 40 years of peace in Europe, itself a direct result of the success of NATO and its basic strategy of non-aggressive deterrence based on the triad of conventional, theatre and strategic nuclear forces, the UK is not going to be easily persuaded that a major overhaul and increase in civil defence is needed. Yet this is what must be done.

A ROLE FOR THE TA

If civil defence is to be treated as part of the totality of the defence of the realm and the bulk of the Regular Army returns to the United Kingdom, this would allow the TA, which would no longer have a major external reinforcement role, being given the civil defence function. What then of the TA? Traditionally it has always been a volunteer force. This is its strength and certainly if the TA ceased to be mainly volunteer its character would change. The TA is not the only source of manpower available to the forces and there are reservists of various classes both for the Royal Navy and Royal Air Force. The essential difference, however, is that whereas the TA produces units other reserve organisations produce men. Even this is not wholly true as in the Naval Reserve a number of ships (units) are manned by reservists. Once the major strategic decision is taken, that the overall contribution to the defence of European NATO that the UK makes should be in strengthening the non-nuclear capabilities of the Northern Region, all else falls into place. The reinforcement role which the TA has had for many years and which, for reasons already adumbrated, is not much more than a charade, will cease. These may seem strong words but the great lesson which constantly comes out of reinforcement exercises by the TA is that the mass movement of non-Regular forces from the UK to battle positions in Germany is simply not a realistic operation of war. The chaos at minor unit and individual level, that these moves in peace-time conditions produce, gives a fair indication as to what would go on in the event of war or rumour of war, assuming of course that the political decision would actually ever be taken to move the TA from the UK. Far better to give the TA a realistic role in peace and war. This will involve a return to its historic mission, the close defence of the United Kingdom itself. This should now include civil defence. In the event of an attack on the UK a 'heavy rescue battalion' will have a role equally important to the survival of the nation as that of an armoured recce squadron. What is needed, besides a massive reorganisation of both the civil defence and home defence forces, is numbers. This will not be achieved by relying on volunteers.

THE LACK OF RESERVES

A major weakness in Britain's defence posture is her lack of trained reserve manpower. Alone of the European powers on either side of the Iron Curtain she is unable to accept casualties. Indeed it could be said that Britain's present defence posture is designed to ensure that she is unable to fight a major war in Europe of any kind. Her defence concept relies almost entirely upon a war in Europe being short. The fact of the matter is that the proportion of the working population of the UK is reducing. One of the side products of this will be that the number of those prepared to volunteer, either for the regular forces or for the TA or reserves, will fall. We are not alone in having this problem. Recently the Federal Republic has extended its call-up period from 15 to 18 months due to the demographic trends in West Germany.[53] In the long term the UK, if it is to produce a viable realistic defence policy, will need to be based upon highly trained and motivated Regular forces backed up by sizeable home based territorial formations with large numbers of reserves who have had some form of military or civil defence training. This will require the reintroduction of some form of National Service.

NATIONAL SERVICE

Senior officers in the Army have nearly always been against National service. Arguments have been put forward that it makes (or would make) the Army less efficient. The role of the Army is not to be a vast training machine but an instrument of war. No doubt some will point to the Falklands campaign as being an example of the results of pitting Regulars against National Servicemen. It is even suggested that equipment these days is so complex that only regulars can have the length of training and experience to operate it. These arguments may have merit. However, it is interesting to note that the early days of the successful Malaysian campaign and the Korean War were fought with National Servicemen, as were the operations in Kenya (Mau Mau) and Cyprus (pre-1960).

However the National Service being suggested is for home and civil defence and would be essentially TA based. The TA itself, and the same applies to the equivalent formations and units of the Navy and Air Force, should have two roles. The first will be a continuation of its relationship with the Regular Army in the provision of formations and units to bring the, now mainly home based, Regular Divisions up to war establishment. The second role will be the training and organisation of a civil defence corps. Clearly the TA alone will not be able to perform this function. The regular home-based army will therefore need to assist in this role by providing the wherewithal to receive and train the National Service intake.

What is envisaged is a system whereby every able bodied man would serve an initial training period in the Army. This initial period would be for, say, six months, when the recruit would receive normal military basic training. However, there should be less emphasis on weapon training than in the past. This would be replaced by the teaching of other skills – first aid, personal survival techniques and team rescue skills, for example. At the end of this initial training the recruit would go either to a TA military unit or to a Territorial Civil Defence Unit to complete his one year National Service. This second part of his training could be sandwiched with his Youth Training Scheme. Indeed the whole basis of the plan would be that the young man having completed his initial training, done by the Regular Army, would continue his National Service at his home town where his civil defence unit will be located.

Such a scheme would require a major change in the concept of defence in the United Kingdom. However, there is no reason that this should not be politically and socially acceptable. If the young Norwegians or Swiss see National Service as a perfectly acceptable duty of citizenship surely youngsters in Britain will feel the same? The charges of militarism and other similar objections to the concept of national service can be answered in the very considerable civil defence emphasis which would be given to the scheme. What the return of some form of compulsory service will produce is an ever increasing pool of reservists, available in the event of war for both military and civil defence units. This would, in time, correct the major and fundamental weakness of the present defence posture of the country; the complete lack of ability to take part in anything other than a short war.

This additional role for the TA would change its *raison d'être* to a great extent. However, there would still be an important, indeed vital, role for the volunteer. What is envisaged is a total change in the defence posture of the UK not only in its home defence but also in its strategic role within NATO. The increased capability for Great Britain to survive attack on the homeland whether from small groups at one extreme to major air attack at the other would be as much an increase to NATO's total defence as, for instance, would be an extra division in Germany or Greece.

TOTALITY IN HOME DEFENCE PLANNING

Home defence, not to be confused with civil defence, would be the responsibility of the regular armed services. As far as the army is concerned, the return to the UK of two divisions would enable more realistic home defence plans to be made.

The TA

Here the TA should be integrated with the Regular divisions, thus allowing them to be increased in size. Each Regular division should consist of two Regular brigades and one TA brigade. On that basis, the actual number of divisions in the order of battle could be increased, with no significant increase in manpower by certainly two, and possibly three, divisions.

The changes and additions needed to increase the effectiveness and security of the air defence network of the country, and at this point it is as well to remember that the UK air defence system is integrated with the overall NATO air defence command structure, are minimal. The commander-in-chief (UK) air is a NATO appointment of major subordinate command status. He is as well a British officer. Fortunately since the publication of the 1984 Defence White Paper the air defence of the country has improved. Although an integrated system the core of the capability is based on aircraft equipped in the interceptor role.

The RAF

The security of the air defence fighter air bases is in the hands of the Royal Air Force Regiment which, in this context, has two tasks; the operation of the close point defence of the bases against air attack. This is based on the Rapier, ground to air guided missile. The second task is to guard against the possibility of ground attack. As these tasks are static, at least in strategic and deployment terms, they should become more and more a role for an increasing Royal Air Force Regiment (Territorial) Reserve which, as with the TA, would be manned by national service men and women, as well as by long term volunteers. As these reservists gain in experience and numbers, so more and more RAF Regiment Regular personnel can be moved to Germany where there is a strong case not only to increase the ground to air defences of the RAF (clutch) air bases in Germany but also to give to the mobile Harrier and support helicopter units greater air defence cover. There is little doubt that these mobile units, because of their tactical flexibility, will be a prime target, if found, for the Warsaw Pact ground attack offensive support fighter aircraft. This is not the only area in which, over a period of time, the creation of a home based national service force will allow for an increase in the overall effectiveness of those British forces stationed on the Continent.

The Royal Navy

The role of the Navy in home defence terms is more difficult to separate, as a task, from its more strategic tasks of sea denial and sea defence. This is in contrast to land and air forces where the division is more clear.

Clearly, however, the security of the UK naval bases, whether they be for the strategic missile carrying submarines through to the in-shore mine counter-measures vessels, is a vital overall requirement. This task though can be carried out by Army and TA units for ground defence and RAF Regiments squadrons for air defence.

As far as the purely naval tasks are concerned there are two, in-shore mine-laying and mine counter-measures, which can become a major role for Naval Reserve units. One of the more ominous results consequent upon the near demise of the deep sea British trawler fleet is the fact that the number of small ships available for this, and other, tasks is becoming less and less. Indeed, if the continuing trend in the reduction of the British fishing fleet continues, existing plans will cease to be viable. As part of the overall strategic defence posture of the UK and as a matter of some urgency the Government needs to review its policy towards the British fishing industry. If a very considerable subsidy is needed to keep this industry viable then it should be given on the grounds not only that it preserves jobs in peace-time but also that, in the event of crisis or war, there is an in-shore fleet of small ships immediately available for operational tasks. Ships without men are as useless as men without ships and it may well be that a job creation scheme to assist in the redevelopment of the British trawler fleet should be started for the same strategic reasons. It is quite clear that the Soviet fishing fleet is used as a peace-time political weapon and already the situation has been reached where a large number of the existing British Fleet depends to some extent on selling their catches to the Russian factory ships. This state of affairs is unsatisfactory, not only for short term economic reasons but also for longer term strategic factors.

PEACETIME STRATEGIC DEFENCE

Home defence must be regarded as a totality. Economic measures to preserve areas of activity which, in strategic terms, are vital must be taken in peace-time even if they might be against the general political mores of any particular Government. Self-sufficiency in food production may not be possible. Nevertheless preferential treatment for British farmers can, or ought to, be justified on strategic grounds. In this respect membership of the European Economic Community (EEC) is working against the long term strategic interests of Britain and therefore of Western Europe (i.e. NATO) itself.

A particular case in point is the introduction of milk quotas imposed upon the United Kingdom by the EEC. These quotas were in fact reductions which, as a result, have meant that from a situation of self-sufficiency in milk production, the total milk herd has been reduced and Britain cannot now produce sufficient milk for itself. Because a milk herd takes years to develop, this specific decision has done immense harm to the defence capability of the country. What is even more extraordinary is that it was a Conservative Government which allowed the situation to develop.

If therefore in future the long term strategic interests of the UK are to be preserved, there should be formed a special Strategic Economic and Defence Sub-Committee. This should be a Prime Minister's Committee with the task of reviewing all measures proposed by any Government Department to see what, if any, strategic defence implications are involved. These sort of questions are obviously asked now in the areas of economic activity – computer technology, defence contracts and so forth. The point is, as the leadership of the Russian Empire well knows and practices, all economic activity is, in the end, strategic. Home defence if it is to be effective as part of the overall deterrent strategy of the United Kingdom must be seen by the British themselves and their allies as realistic. It must also be perceived by any potential aggressor as effective. This can only be achieved if the population as a whole is involved.

10 The Deployment and Organisation of the Regular Forces

IMPLICATIONS OF NATIONAL SERVICE

The reintroduction of National Service in the form suggested will allow for an expansion of the Regular forces. Like the TA, the military NS man, as opposed to the majority who will serve in the civil defence NS, would serve his time in the UK. There is little doubt that once National Service was introduced a significant number would go for the military National Service option. A choice of enrolment would be given – CD or military NS. As with the civil defence, after the initial basic training period, the NS man would, as far as possible, serve his time in a formation based close to his home. His part-time TA service would certainly be with a unit stationed near his home or place of work. This would allow for the much needed expansion in the use of reservists, thus releasing the full-time professionals for those specific roles more suited to the skills and training capital expended these days on the Regular. The suggestion that a greater use should be made of reservists is not new. The Omega Report published in 1983 clearly adumbrated the shortcomings inherent in the UK's present defence policies. The shortage of reservists places considerable incredulity upon the ability of the UK to fight any type of war except one that is limited and short (the Falklands). Even the existing reservists, despite the improvements that have taken place over the past two years, have serious shortcomings not only in numbers (and this will get worse as the demographic trends of an increasingly elderly population continue) but also in training time, which means that as efficient fighting men they have some way to go.

Two quotations from this report are sufficient to make the point:

> The volunteer reserve forces are too small, and their structure is unbalanced, making them unsuitable for the military threats now facing NATO in general and Britain in particular.[54]
>
> Britain needs to restructure and increase her reserve forces, particu-

larly her naval and air reserves, and to allocate more of them to roles connected with the *defence of the NATO Northwestern flank* to which reference has been made.[55] [Author's emphasis]

The point is that the reduction of Britain's service manpower representing as it does in the period 1972–82 a loss in manpower terms of some 12.9 per cent [56] with, at the same time, the maintenance of major roles in Germany and the North Atlantic, as well as the home defence and the training roles inherent in any defence policy, has now spread the military commitment far too thin. The increasing importance of the NATO Northern Region and its relatively worsening position, in military terms, to the overwhelming maritime threat, with all that this implies, makes it essential that not only does Britain reintroduce some form of conscription but that her regular forces are made much more efficient use of, in strategic terms.

The whole concept of part-time reservists has been under debate. Yet, however attractive terms are made, there will ever only be a certain proportion of men and women prepared to volunteer. This is the essential weakness in all plans based on the volunteer principle. As the all-Regular British Armed Forces need to retain a credibility with their allies they must be able to sustain prolonged operations if there was to be a war in Europe. They must therefore be backed up by sufficient reservist manpower which is itself sufficiently well trained and practised so that the casualities inevitable in war can be quickly replaced. The single scenario short war is all very well but it fails to address the problem of the scenario being wrong. What is worse is that it allows politicians to continue fooling themselves that all is well.

In broad terms these National Service men and reservists would take on those roles in which it would be most economic and realistic for them to do so. Other than certain selected TA units, no NS and reserve unit would serve overseas nor would there be plans for them to do so. Once this is accepted the charade that TA units would ever be able to move at the drop of a hat and actually fight can be dispensed with. The roles clearly which came most quickly to mind are:

(a) In the case of the Royal Navy:
   (1) Mine counter-measures units,
   (2) Port and facility defences,
   (3) In-shore small craft operations,
   (4) Merchant shipping,
   (5) Manning of 'moth-balled' frigates (together with Regulars),
   (6) Volunteers with Commando forces.

(b) In the case of the Army and TA:
  (1) Point and area defence of key installations,
  (2) Home based TA brigades with home defence tasks,
  (3) Specialised volunteer units and individuals (SAS, Commando forces, helicopter units),
  (4) Logistics units,
  (5) Field hospitals,
  (6) Airfield repair units (Royal Engineers).

(c) In the case of the Royal Air Force:
  (1) Manning of anti-aircraft missile and gun units on *all* airfields,
  (2) Point and ground defence units of all airfields,
  (3) Manning of transport aircraft squadrons

THE REDEPLOYMENT AND ORGANISATION OF THE ARMY

The change of emphasis in the proposals that have been adumbrated will have the greatest effect on the Army. At present the peace-time deployment within the NATO area of responsibility of battalion sized units is as follows:

In the UK 53 (including army air corps and training battalions)
In Germany 50 (including army air corps)[57]

To those units based in the UK can be added the three Royal Marines Commandoes which are battalion equivalents plus a logistic unit.

This commitment in peace-time to the Central Region is at the expense of producing a more realistic and immediate response capability in the Northern Region and must now be severely reduced. In a previous chapter the proposal has been made of a cut from three divisions plus artillery and other support units to one division at near war establishment plus an artillery division and other support units.

FOUR MAJOR PROPOSALS

To allow for a significant shifting of Britain's commitments within NATO to the Northern Region. Specifically it is proposed that:

(a) The contingency reinforcements to Jutland be increased from a Light Brigade to a Three Brigade Light Division.

(b) A contingency plan for reinforcement of south Norway of a Two Brigade Light Division should be developed.
(c) The contingency reinforcements for north Norway to be increased from the present Commando Brigade to a two Brigade Task Force (one Commando, one Parachute Brigade).
(d) The existing home defence formations will, with the reintroduction of NS, be larger and a major restructuring of mixed Regular/TA divisions can occur. All brigades should be mixed. That is to say regular brigades would have at least one TA battalion sized unit, whilst TA heavy brigades would have at least one Regular battalion sized unit. The army takes on the training commitment for all NS intakes both for the CD and military streams. The bulk of the TA in the meantime will take on CD roles (heavy and light rescue, monitoring, first aid and survival units as well as communications).

IMPLICATIONS OF THE NORTH NORWAY CONTINGENCY

Of all the commitments to which British forces are at present allocated the most fraught is the reinforcement of north Norway. Not only is the threat posed by the Soviet Fleet formidable and there is the need for such a reinforcement force not only to have to fight its way to the area of concern, but the land/air threat is, even without the Northern Fleet, of considerable significance. There is therefore the need for such a force to be able to conduct sustained operations once ashore. These difficulties are recognised and the importance of the real estate referred to as north Norway was emphasised in the Defence White Paper 1985:

> NATO's Northern Flank is of vital importance to the integrity of the Alliance and to the conduct of maritime operations in the Norwegian Sea and Atlantic as well as to the UK itself. We therefore commit substantial resources to the defence of the Region.[58]

The proposal is that these forces should be a great deal more substantial. This can only be done by a redeployment of Britain's military effort from the Central Region to the Northern Area.

However, the sheer effort expended in merely surviving in the Arctic Region requires highly trained and motivated troops. This is not a place for part-time soldiers. Other than the Norwegians the best in the business are the British and Canadians. The Canadians' contribution must be taken into account and there is little doubt that, if a proportion of this particular force could be stationed in Scotland, this would make a great deal of difference to the reality of some of the contingency planning.

Ideally what ought to be done is for a multinational Divisional Headquarters (British/Canadian) to be located in the UK. It would be responsible to the two governments and to the responsible NATO commanders (SACLANT, SACEUR at MNC level, CINCEASTLANT and CINCNORTH at MSC level) for the contingency planning for the reinforcement of, and operations in, north Norway. This division would have under its operational command or control, the Canadian Regimental Combat Team, the Commando Brigade and the (reformed) Parachute Brigade.

Short of the ideal should be a new British division (the assault division) consisting of:

Parachute Brigade (two parachute and one air landed battalion groups)
Commando Brigade (three commando groups)
SAS Regiment

The Headquarters staff would have Army and RM officers and men and could be commanded by a marine or soldier. This would actually give an operational appointment of general rank in peace to the Royal Marines, which strangely, they have not actually had, certainly since 1945.

Implicit in this proposal is that the Parachute Brigade is reformed as such and that there should again be an operational capability of dropping in one lift a complete battalion group. (A battalion group is a battalion plus its supporting artillery and engineer support.) The reason that the SAS is included is that this division would, in effect, be the formation for all British Special forces and, as such, could be responsible for the planning and carrying out of all 'out of the NATO area' contingencies.

OUT OF AREA OPERATIONS

Britain still needs the capability of major combined operations out of area and also needs to be able to conduct such operations with or without allies. The creation of the assault division will go a long way to fill the gap once occupied by the 3rd Division, the old strategic reserve formation.

NEW TASKS FOR THE EX-BAOR DIVISIONS

The two divisions that return from Germany will each have separate reinforcement roles in the Northern Region. One will be for operations in Jutland where at present contingencies exist for a single brigade. As the potential threat to this area north of the Elbe is part and parcel of the major land/air threat from East Germany. This strengthening of the defending land forces north of the Elbe will take some of the strain off the German Army. Indeed, such a visible sign that the proposed shift is within NATO and not out of NATO should make the whole exercise more acceptable to the Germans. It will certainly be acceptable to the Danes and Norwegians.

The other division on its return from Germany should have a primary home defence role. However, a realistic secondary role will be to develop contingencies to reinforce NATO forces in the south of Norway. Norway's problem is that many of her units are in the south and she will need to move a large proportion of them to the north. In any event the longitudinal length of that country poses many problems for her defence planners, particularly if it becomes apparent that Swedish neutrality might be violated. A major strategic aim on the part of the Soviet Union could be to cut off the more populated south Norway from its less populated, but extremely valuable in strategic terms, Northern Territories. A reinforcement contingency of a British Light Division could, in these circumstances, be extremely valuable to NATO and Norwegian national planners.

PROPOSALS FOR THE ROYAL NAVY

As the Eastern Flank of the United States Navy and the most sizeable naval force operating in the European NATO Northern Region, the contribution that the Royal Navy has made and is still making to NATO defence plans is immense. However, the time has come when it is now very doubtful whether or not it is capable of fulfilling its commitments. The greatest danger, since the introduction of the 'flexible response' strategy, is that the low level of conventional forces in the Northern Region could lead, at some time in the future, to the

USSR leadership miscalculating NATO's response to a limited military aggression. Deterrence is maintained not only by a nuclear capability but also, and in some ways in a more important way, by conventional forces. Conventional deterrence is much less easy to define and certainly less easy to calculate.

Unlike the Central Region, most of the Northern Area is sea. A fleet can move at will on the high seas. Unlike armies it can move to an area of strategic importance and without a single act against international law render an area, a vital area, strategically impotent. The need therefore for strong maritime forces, both naval and air, particularly in the Northern Region has become vital if NATO is to retain an all-round equilibrium of defensive capability.

The centre with its obvious confrontational posture which includes, whether the British Corps was there or not, conventional forces of considerable strength as well as nuclear forces armed with short and medium range weapons is not the area for non-nuclear 'try it on' adventures. The presence of the Americans in strength with two Corps and the powerful United States Air Forces Europe make a limited non-nuclear military aggression so unlikely that it can be almost discounted. In the south, the presence of the US 6th Fleet with its strike carriers render the possibility of a Soviet maritime adventure equally unlikely. It is to the Northern Region that Soviet planners will look if they wish to change the politico/military situation to their advantage with the least risk of a nuclear response from NATO. It is this which makes it so desperately important that NATO increases its maritime forces in this area.

Britain, because of her geographical position, is uniquely fitted to take on this role, and take it on she must, even at the cost of an angry West Germany. The maritime threat to Britain is as real, as immediate, and as dangerous to her, as the land/air threat from Eastern Europe and western Russia is real, immediate, and dangerous to Western Germany. If a massive increase in defence expenditure is to be discounted, there is no alternative option.

Therefore there needs to be a shifting of budgetary effort from maintaining BAOR at present levels (most of which it must be said is in foreign currency) to a build up of Britain's naval, air and maritime forces. The reductions proposed in the 1981 White Paper must not be implemented. The total of destroyers and frigates will have to be increased as will the size and carrying capacity of the Royal Navy's amphibious shipping. What is needed is 'cheap and nasties' for the troops and a maximum weapons capacity for the escorts.

Certainly the major, non-nuclear strategic arm of the Royal Navy its attack (fleet) submarines needs to be increased. If the surface fleet is also to be increased, as it must be, this will, as has already been suggested, require a much higher proportion of reservists. Virtually all the smaller ships could be largely reservist manned. However, one area in which the Royal Navy can be helped is in the weaponry with which it is supplied. A surface launched weapon only needs a platform from which to be launched. Whether or not a ship-to-ship missile is launched from an aircraft carrier, destroyer or frigate makes no difference to its effect at the other end.

The use of hovercraft and hydrofoils as weapons platforms should be investigated. Five large hovercraft armed with guns and missiles would cost the same as three frigates and would have not only greater fire power and tactical flexibility but also greater survivability. Clearly the North Sea is not the same environment as the Gulf of Mexico or Pacific but the US Navy is now making considerable use of both those types of ship. Indeed, the US 'Navy's most potent warships on the basis of fire power per displacement ton'[59] are its hydrofoils. Operating as inshore squadrons and manned by reservists, a mixed force of small ships, hovercraft and hydrofoils would be an extremely valuable deterrent force against major amphibious assault right through the spectrum to sea landed small commando group operations.

The major weakness at present is the ability of the Royal Navy to sustain operations outside the NATO territory. The Falklands campaign was a brilliant success but if present trends continue, the UK will cease to have this particular military capability. Even if this option was dropped, the situation is now being reached where even our NATO commitments are in danger. The present Government has at least recognised this in part: 'It is of concern that, if the decline continues for several more years at the present rate, it could become increasingly difficult for us to discharge at least some of our NATO obligations.'[60]

The decline referred to is in the tonnage of the UK Merchant Fleet. If these comments can be made in a White Paper which is a political document the situation must be bad indeed. The Merchant Fleet of the UK cannot be allowed to decline. Not only are there powerful economic arguments for its retention but the strategic case for ensuring that the UK has its own Merchant Marine capable of sustaining the national interests is overwhelming. As part of the defence effort, therefore, it will be necessary to subsidise the major British shipowners not only in the building of merchant ships in

British Yards but even to subsidising their running costs. The innate loyalty of the merchant seamen to the UK was amply demonstrated during the Falklands campaign. To a man they volunteered and the success of the whole operation was due as much to the efforts of the merchant seamen as it was to the individual officers and men who fought ashore. The UK needs to harness their efforts as much in peace as in war. The observable capability of the Merchant Marine to sustain the UK in the event of war, and this will only happen if deterrence fails, is part and parcel of the whole panoply of the non-nuclear deterrent posture of this country. Any area of observable weakness in operational capability weakens the whole deterrent strategy. This area is one which must be put right with the added advantage that there will be immediate peace-time advantages accruing therefrom, the production of jobs in one of our strategic industrial industries – shipbuilding.

PROPOSALS FOR THE ROYAL AIR FORCE

The need for a radical change in budgetary expenditure for the Royal Air Force is not so great as for the other two services. The inherent flexibility of air power with its ability to project force over long distances concentrated if necessary at the desired area in time and sorties makes the need for redeployment less urgent. However, as a political signal, the reduction in the strength of BAOR could be accompanied by an increase in the deployed strength of RAF squadrons in Germany.

In this respect the proposal is the opposite of that proposed in the Omega Report, which suggests a reduction in RAF (G). However, the intention for NATO to develop a tactical doctrine which aims at increasing the capability of the Allied Tactical Air Forces to hit at WP follow-up land formations is so important that Britain's continuing involvement as a major contributor to the military power of the Central Region is vital. This then should be Britain's major contribution – air power, particularly in the ground support role.

The air defence of Great Britain is part of the overall NATO Air Defence System. Recent improvements in this capability will be continued. However, the introduction of NS and the increase of reservist strength will enable the RAF, over a period of time, to redeploy much of its professional officer and manpower strength into those areas better served by Regulars – the fighter ground and interceptor roles in particular as well as the overseas manned squadrons.

Much more use should be made of professional air-line pilots, all of whom should have a secondary role as part-time Royal Auxiliary Air Force pilots. There is no reason why all the existing transport support squadrons should not be manned by mixed Regular and auxiliary pilots. Agreements should be made with the British airlines so that cross-posting of pilots can occur on a planned long-term basis.

The expansion of, in particular, short-range air defence (SHORAD) has already been alluded to. There is little doubt that the 'knock on' effect of NS and reservists taking on these roles in ever increasing numbers will be considerable in the other areas of air operations.

As stated in the Omega Report:

> a major additional benefit would undoubtedly be the improved integration of the dedicated but sometimes isolated service personnel with the local civilian community. Whilst leaving the bulk of the RDF commitment to professional servicemen and to the Royal Auxiliary Air Force pilots, the home-based Royal Auxiliary Air Force Squadron and support personal *would provide a highly cost-effective means of meeting the new Northwestern Flank Task.*[61] [Author's emphasis]

SUMMARY

The redeployment of the Army in particular together with the introduction of NS will enhance the whole strategic posture of Great Britain. Although most of the NS intake will serve in the civil defence role sufficient will do their time in the armed services to allow many of the home defence roles to be taken on by TA and reserve units. This in turn will strengthen the Regular Forces in those roles for which they are best fitted – offensive operations.

The creation of an all-Regular assault division with the associated increases in amphibious shipping and air lift capability will ensure that Britain is able to maintain a significant 'out of NATO' capability, able to operate with or without allies. None of this will be possible without the retention of a large British Merchant Marine.

Defence is the concern of everyone and the emphasis placed on CD as being as much a part of the overall defence of the country as is the defence of airfields and ports will make NS, once more, an acceptable part of the normal duties and rights of citizenship. The ability of Britain, as a vital partner in NATO, to counter the hitherto relatively ignored but growing threat to the Northern Region is essential to the future overall deterrent posture of NATO. As part of this response to the changing nature of the Soviet non-nuclear strategic threat, Britain must reduce her land force commitment to the Central Region. Such a redeployment of forces, however, must not be used as an excuse to reduce present levels of defence expenditure.

11 Statement on the Defence Estimates 198?

Each year the Government presents to Parliament the Defence Estimates for the following year. They are presented in two parts. Part I is a political document and consists of a series of essays setting out the background, as perceived by the Government, to the strategic scene and the general way in which it has reached its conclusions as to how the defence of the country should be organised. Part II is a more technical document and presents the financial consequences of the policies laid out in Part I. A change in Part II will be a consequence of an alteration of defence policy in Part I. The obverse does not apply.

The 1984 Defence Estimates, Part I as presented consisted of five chapters and a series of annexes and diagrams amplifying the subject matter in the main chapters. These had the following headings:

Chapter 1 Defence Policy
Chapter 2 Management of Defence
Chapter 3 Equipment Procurement
Chapter 4 Force Capabilities
Chapter 5 The Services and the Community

Of these chapters, the first and the fourth dealt with the heart of the Government's defence strategy. As a summary therefore of the arguments in the previous chapters the book will end with the essays that a future Government should present to Parliament in two future Chapters 1 and 4. As the actual comparative 'force strengths' figures change from year to year the essays will be conceptual rather than detailed.

The subheadings within the two chapters will be those actually used in the 1984 White Paper, Part 1.

A DEFENCE WHITE PAPER 198?

Chapter 1 Defence Policy

The North Atlantic Treaty Organisation which is the visible expression of the Western democracies' continuing political coherence remains, as it has done since 1949, the keystone of Britain's defence strategy.

> As a Government we continue to believe that the collective security which we enjoy as members of the Alliance is the only realistic way of providing for our defence. We therefore remain committed to playing our full part in ensuring that NATO continues to be as effective a guarantor of peace and freedom in the decades ahead as it has in the years since 1949.[62]

The challenge facing NATO

'When the North Atlantic Treaty was signed, the threat was direct and immediate. Berlin was under blockade.'[63] The threat today may appear to be less immediate. It is, however, direct and in some respects more dangerous. The nature of the original threat has changed in two respects. The Soviet Union has become a nuclear power and her strategic and tactical nuclear capability is at least the equal of, and in some areas greater than that of the United States. The rise of the Red Navy from being basically a defensive fleet to that of a strategic blue water fleet, with a submarine force of over 400 boats with both nuclear powered, and nuclear armed, submarines as well as a surface fleet including carriers, represents a strategic threat of worldwide proportions to NATO. The Alliance must continue to base its defensive posture on Soviet capabilities and not on her declared intentions. In this respect it must be said that the whole pattern of Soviet and Warsaw Pact force improvements demonstrates a continuing and improving capability for offensive operations.

'Existing superiorities over NATO forces have been maintained, and in many cases increased.'[64] The Soviet Union has continued her deployment of SS20 missiles which now constitute a direct political and military threat, not only to the whole of Western Europe, but to all the Arab States, the Indian subcontinent and continental Asia. The modest NATO response in the positioning of Cruise and Pershing II missiles in Europe including, in the case of Cruise, the UK has and is still taking place. This programme is still open to reversal if the Soviet Union agrees to, and begins, the actual dismantling of her SS20 missiles.

The picture in terms of general military capabilities remains much the same. The steady increase in Soviet military capability in every significant category of armament, conventional and nuclear commented upon in the 1984 Defence White Paper has continued. 'At sea, it now has the largest fleet of nuclear-powered submarines in the world.'[65] On land, particularly in the Central Region the overwhelming superiority of the Warsaw Pact in tanks and artillery still represents a military threat of a most formidable kind. In the air, the operational capabilities of her long range bombers, Bear, Bison and Backfire, backed up with Badger and Blinder, continue to pose a strategic threat, whilst at the tactical level her Fishbed, Flogger, Fitter and Fencer aircraft, some 3000 in number, enhance the offensive capability of Soviet and WP land forces.

Besides the nuclear and conventional capabilities of the Soviet Union she has one other military capability to add to the sum total of her non-nuclear power, that of chemical warfare. The Soviet Union has continued research, development and manufacture of chemical agents. The NATO estimate which appeared in the 1984 White Paper that the Soviet Union had chemical weapons stocks of some 300 000 tonnes is still realistic. It must be emphasised that this fire power is contained in stocks of modern warheads. Soviet and WP land forces continually train in the offensive use of these weapons. The time is approaching when NATO and the UK may well have to rethink their common approach to this growing threat. Of the NATO powers only the US has stocks of offensive chemical weapons and these are ageing, a reflection of the self-imposed moratorium on the manufacture of chemical weapons which the US placed upon herself in 1965. These weapons are not declared to NATO.

It is our firm hope that the negotiations on the banning of all chemical weapons, in which Her Majesty's Government is playing a leading role and to which the Soviet Government is a party, will lead to positive and verifiable reductions in this class of weapon. However, if these negotiations fail this may mean that, in order to build up a realistic deterrent against the use of chemical weapons, the NATO powers will have to reconsider their position on the matter of chemical offensive weaponry. In the meantime, the UK will continue the development of defensive measures including monitoring techniques, medical counter-weapons and of protective clothing. All new vehicles, aircraft and ships will have built into them filter and overpressure systems to enable them to operate in the chemical environment.

Arms control

A fundamental aim behind the deterrent policy followed by NATO and Her Majesty's Government is the reduction of all weapons and the elimination of some. Despite the evidence that the Soviet Union continues to strengthen its capabilities in both nuclear and non-nuclear weaponry, NATO still believes that meaningful negotiations can take place. Bilateral negotiations between the US and USSR on the levels of their strategic nuclear weapons are fully supported by Her Majesty's Government. Mutual and Balanced Force Reductions (MBFR) negotiations are immensely complicated as a balance has to be struck between the tactical capabilities of 'in place' forces against the reinforcement times and strengths of units in western and central Russia against, on the other hand, US reinforcements which can arrive by air, with a limited fighting capability, or by sea, with the consequent time penalty.

In the nuclear field it is the Government's view that some significant progress must be made in the levels of the strategic nuclear forces before realistic negotiations on intermediate and short range nuclear weapons can start. However, the Government is prepared to include its own nuclear weapons in any future negotiations once success has attended the present US–USSR talks.

The continuing deployment of Cruise missiles in Europe is now sufficiently far advanced, for NATO to reappraise its doctrine on the role of its short range land based tactical nuclear weapons (Lance, Honest John and guns).

This class of weapon because of its short range is potentially vulnerable. Her Majesty's Government intends therefore to press her NATO allies that this particular class of weapon should be phased out of the NATO inventory. The tasks, tactical strikes against military targets in or near the immediate battle area, at present allotted to these weapons, should be taken over by units armed with Cruise missiles. This will remove from the battle area the most vulnerable of all NATO nuclear weapons. It will also be a unilateral reduction by NATO of a complete class of nuclear weapons whilst still allowing NATO forces to retain, as part of its deterrent posture, an observable tactical nuclear capability.

Developments in NATO's defence posture

Whilst there have been many improvements in NATO in the standardisation of weapons, commonality of procedures, host nation support, the sharing of development costs and so forth, unit costs of major items of equipment, aircraft, tanks, ships, etc., are still much higher than for the Warsaw Pact. The Alliance has remained, in strategic terms relatively static in the face of a military and political threat which itself is continuing to develop and, in one respect, has changed and changed fundamentally. This is in the emergence of the threat from the North.[66] Not only is NATO faced in the Central Region by a formidable land/air military threat but over the years there has grown up a massive maritime threat. The Soviet Northern Fleet, with its ancillary units, located at its five bases on the Kola Peninsula, Severornsk, Motovshij, Gremikla, Polyarny and Archangelsk represents the most powerful single concentration of naval power in the world. Not only does this force include over 180 submarines, of which over 40 are nuclear-powered, like the Delta and Typhoon classes, but the surface fleet of over 200 ships including aircraft carriers of the Kiev class and destroyers gives this fleet the capability of attempting to impose its military will in the Norwegian Sea with a high probability of success. NATO, despite recent exercises by the Striking Fleet Atlantic in the Arctic area, if present trends continue will be hard pressed to even deny the Eastern Atlantic to the Red Navy.

This fleet is further backed up by Soviet naval aviation squadrons comprising at least 310 combat aircraft which include TU-26 Backfires, TU-16 Badgers and TU-22 Blinder supersonic bombers. From the 40 or so airfields in the Kola Peninsula the Soviet Union possess the capability of attacking anywhere in Norway, Sweden and Denmark in support of maritime and/or land operations. There are, besides these maritime and air forces, a total of seven Soviet divisions, numbering some 70 000 men deployed in the Kola Peninsula. The Soviet Union also has the capability of dropping certainly one, and possibly two, airborne divisions anywhere from North Norway to Jutland in support of, or supported by, maritime and/or land/air operation against Norway or Denmark.

Unlike the Central Region, where although NATO is weaker than the Warsaw Pact she is at least observably strong, in the north, NATO in relative terms, has become, and is still becoming weaker.[67]

This relative weakness is a growing area of danger as the Soviet leadership might be tempted to change the political balance, to neutralise Norway for instance, by the application of military power. NATO, as a matter of urgency must address itself to this strategic problem. As this threat is a direct one upon the UK because of this country's unique geographical position, Her Majesty's Government intends to open negotiations with NATO with the aim of effecting a fundamental change in the strategic defensive posture of the UK within NATO. Essentially the Government believes that the UK must adopt a basically maritime strategy and as a result its main defensive effort must be directed towards the strengthening of NATO's European Northern Region. The UK already supplies a NATO commander, a major subordinate commander status (MSC) Commander-in-Chief Northern Region (CINCNORTH).

The time has now come that there should be an increase in the forces available for the defence of this vital region.

The United Kingdom – contribution to NATO

The UK has no intention of reducing its present level of forces allocated to NATO. She does, however, feel that, as the major NATO European maritime power, it will best serve the future strategic needs of NATO by directing the major part of her defence effort to the security of the eastern Atlantic, the Channel, the Norwegian Sea and North Sea and in the provision of land and air forces to the defence of Norway and Denmark. This can be done only by an increase in defence spending, which the Government feels unable to recommend, or by a redisposing of resources from the centre to the north. It is therefore the Government's intention, in conjunction with her NATO allies, to negotiate this realignment of resources. This shift of military power may well require a change in the present NATO command structure.

Northern Ireland

The Government remains committed to the concept of the Union of Great Britain and Northern Ireland. Within that context it will co-operate with the Government of the Southern Ireland Republic to bring to an end the reign of terror which has been conducted both in the south and north of Ireland. British Forces will still be stationed on a permanent basis in Ulster supplemented by 'short tour' visits by UK and German based units.

The Royal Ulster Constabulary (RUC) will continue to receive every support as will the Ulster Defence Regiment (UDR).

Recruiting into these organisations of both Protestant and Catholics from the north will be actively encouraged. There can be no military solution to the problems of Northern Ireland. However, no political solution of any sort will be permitted by the UK Government so long as an active terrorist threat is seen to be influencing the local people whether Protestant, Catholic, or if they are for the continuing relationship with Great Britain or against such a relationship.

Beyond the NATO area

'Though our primary commitment must remain to the North Atlantic Alliance, the threat we face is not limited to the NATO area as defined in the treaty.'[68]

The continuing war between Iraq and Iran may well begin to have a significant effect upon the flow of oil to the Industrial West. The worldwide threat now posed by the Red Navy, supported by the Russian Merchant Marine directed from the Ministry of Defence in Moscow which is at present being used as a strategic economic weapon, is one to which NATO and the UK must be able to respond. In a following chapter we describe how we intend that these 'out of area' responsibilities are and will be, discharged.

However, we recognise that we, as a medium sized military power, cannot continue to do everything and, as a consequence of this, we believe that our future emphasis on a maritime base with the bulk of our land forces being air or sea mobile, will improve our 'out of area' capabilities. This improvement in our worldwide capabilities will strengthen NATO's own strategic position. To this end, not only will negotiation be conducted with our NATO allies, but we will enter into discussions with the US, Australia and New Zealand as to how best our common worldwide maritime interests can be served in the decades to come.

Chapter 4 Force Capabilities

Nuclear forces

British strategic nuclear forces. Britain's current strategic nuclear force of four Polaris submarines has provided a continuous independent deterrent since 1969.[69]

This force, having undergone improvements, specifically with the Chevaline which is designed to give a penetration capability to the system against anti-ballistic missile defences, will remain, in the

Government's view, an effective part of the overall NATO nuclear deterrent posture until well into the 1990s. The Trident programme is designed as an effective system.

However, although in terms of money costs the Trident programme is extremely cost effective, only 3 per cent of the increase in defence expenditure planned since 1984 over the next decade, the Government has reviewed its role within the whole concept of deterrent strategy. We therefore intend to stop the Trident programme and modify the boats intended for the Trident missiles. The Government believes that an independently controlled nuclear deterrent force only makes sense within the context of a continuing, vibrant and strong North Atlantic Alliance. The bedrock of NATO's nuclear deterrence lies with the American Strategic Nuclear Forces and their undoubted second strike capability. This capability is the ultimate deterrent. In this context therefore there is no need for the UK to have a force with similar characteristics as it can, of itself, add nothing to the ultimate deterrent.

However a deterrent to be effective needs a number of levels of response capability and it is at the lower (or earlier) levels of nuclear deterrent that the UK can, indeed ought to, contribute to NATO's nuclear deterrence. The aim of all deterrents, and this includes nuclear as well as conventional forces, is to deter military aggression of any kind whether major or limited. Clearly a massive strategic nuclear response might be perceived to be inappropriate in the case of a limited non-nuclear military aggression. Equally if such a limited aggression took place deterrence has failed. In such a case deterrent power might well have to be used either to contain the aggression or to persuade the aggressor that NATO, contrary to the aggressor's belief, is prepared to increase the level of conflict.

This level of deterrence to be effective needs therefore an observable tactical nuclear capability. This aspect of deterrent will be enhanced if there are NATO powers other than the United States that can trigger this level of nuclear force. This is referred to as the 'second decision centre' concept. It is the Government's belief that this second decision centre concept, and both the UK and France (a full NATO member although not within the peace-time military structure) possess this capability.

The Government believes that this capability will be effective so long as the UK retains a nuclear strike capacity which is relatively invulnerable against a first strike. It is therefore the intention of the Government to retain and modernise as needed her existing air launched tactical nuclear weapons. Future attack aircraft will be designed to be strike/attack.

British theatre nuclear systems. It is therefore the intention that, in addition to the Tornado strike/attack squadrons, the UK will take over the manning of the Cruise missile units in the UK. Already the RAF Regiment supplies the manpower for the security units. We believe that, in time, the Cruise missiles should be jointly manned by UK and US personnel and that by the time Polaris is phased out, the Cruise missiles, or their successors, will be manned and controlled by the UK. The Trident submarines will be modified to accept Cruise missiles and the RAF will, in time, be equipped with the air launched version. The security therefore in the 1990s of the British independently controlled nuclear deterrent force will be in the variety of launch platforms, ground, sea and air. Its effectiveness will be in the observable capability that Britain will retain of being able to initiate a tactical nuclear response to a military aggression, whether limited or major. A consequence of this posture will be an even greater importance in maintaining a strong NATO with the United States remaining the major sustaining power of the Alliance.[70]

Conventional forces

Defence of the United Kingdom. 'Protection of our own country and its people must lie at the heart of our defence policy. It is sound strategy to meet the threat as far from our shores as possible'[71] As we have already discussed the nature of the threat has changed. If the Scandinavian countries should fall into the hands of the Soviet Union, whether or not there has been an attack against the NATO Central Region, the UK would be vulnerable to air attack or airborne invasion, without the advantage that the Air Defence belt deployed in the Central Region gives to our other NATO allies, France, Belgium, the Netherlands and West Germany. If Norway or Denmark should ever become neutralised, the direct threat posed by the Soviet Northern Fleet would become overwhelming. To avoid either of these possibilities, the Government intends to strengthen its reinforcement capabilities in support of the Allied Forces Northern Region Command, specifically for tasks in north Norway and Jutland.

If the United Kingdom is to change its basic defence strategy to concentrate upon a maritime and home defence concept without significantly weakening NATO, two things must happen. Those forces stationed permanently on the European mainland must be at manning and equipment levels so that they can fight effectively without relying upon external reinforcements. Secondly, much more use must be made of reservists in the home base so that the maximum utility can be obtained from the Regular men and women in all three services.

To that end we intend to reintroduce limited National Service and to combine civil and home defence. The responsibility of the Civil Defence Corps, its training, organisation and operational planning will become the responsibility of the Ministry of Defence.

The National Service intended will be shorter than during the last time it was in use in 1946–61. Basically everyone will serve for a six months' initial training period in either a civil defence orientated training unit or a home defence orientated training establishment. Training in either event will become the responsibility of the Regular Army. At the end of the six months' training period the National Servicemen will then serve another year in a TA unit (or Royal Naval Reserve unit or Royal Auxiliary Air Force squadron) near his home. In the case of the TA, which as well as its present military role will take on the civil defence role, these units will either be civil or home defence. On enlistment the recruit may choose, subject to the manpower needs of the country, in which Service he wishes to serve. The Royal Naval and RAAF recruits will all have volunteered for the military role. The year's part-time service will be sandwiched with YTS, polytechnic, university or other specialist educational courses. By this means it is intended that not only will Britain's home and civil defence become much more realistic, but as time goes on a bank of reservists who have had disciplined training will be available if ever a need should arise.

The TA in the meantime will have been considerably enlarged and a number of Regulars will be seconded to the TA to enable it to take on its new and enhanced role. Other than a few specialist units and individuals the TA will not have a specifically planned overseas reinforcement role. The costs of this scheme need to be set against the present costs of maintaining our three million in unemployment benefit and the costs of the existing YTS scheme.

The present level of naval forces will be increased. The UK amphibious forces sea-lift capability will be enhanced. A design project will be started to investigate the feasibility of mini-carriers. These will be ships designed to take VTOL aircraft (Sea Harriers and helicopters) with the minimum of on board servicing facilities.

These ships will be intended to operate with the ASW carriers and by being able to accept fixed-wing aircraft will enhance the operational capabilities of the carriers. One of the lessons of the Falklands campaign is that two carriers on station is not enough. The introduction of up to four mini-carriers will not only increase the operational efficiency of the Royal Navy in its NATO role, but will also ensure that any future 'out of area' operations would be less fraught, in terms of available air support, than the Falklands operation.

The inshore and off-shore flotillas will be increased and research will be conducted into the feasibility of using small craft, including hovercraft and hydrofoils armed with ship-to-ship missiles and manned by reservists for offensive patrol tasks against surface task forces.

We have now become extremely concerned at the strategic implications of the run-down of the Merchant Navy. Already a programme of replacing, by wastage, the non-British personnel manning the Royal Fleet Auxiliaries with British merchant seamen, has started. This will continue. However the need to retain, in peace-time, a viable 'Red Duster' Merchant Fleet is a strategic necessity. To this end therefore the Government will enter negotiations with the opeators and builders to ensure, if necessary by subsidy, that the British Merchant Service remains large enough so that major sustained maritime operations anywhere in the world can be carried out by the UK. This is a strategic option which no responsible British Government could allow to disappear.

The Land Forces whose main roles will now be the defence of the homeland in its widest sense and the reinforcement of the Northern Region will be reorganised. Two complete divisions and one airmobile brigade, 6 Brigade, will be phased back to the UK. These divisions will become light divisions. One, stationed in SE and East England, will have the primary role moving to and operating in Denmark and Jutland, under the operational control of the appropriate NATO commander, in this case Commander Land Forces Jutland (COMLANDJUT). For this role it will consist of two light brigades and one airmobile brigade (6 Brigade). It will have a secondary home defence role. The other to be stationed in NE England and SE Scotland will have a primary home defence role and a secondary reinforcement role to south Norway. It will consist of two light Regular brigades and one TA brigade.

The Regular and TA brigades at present in the UK will be reorganised into divisions and, in the case of the civil defence, into 'area' and 'district' commands. These will be the civil defence equivalents to divisions and brigades. The sixteen brigade headquarters in the UK will come under divisions. These already exist in the form of District Headquarters. The intention will be to have a mixture of Regular heavy brigades (i.e. two Regular battalion-sized units to one TA unit) and TA heavy brigades. The civil defence formations will all be 'TA' heavy, each with Regular Army training cadres which will supply the backbone of the training expertise.

The qualitative and quantitative improvements in UK air defences has continued and involves, as stated in the 1984 White Paper, the replacement or modernisation of virtually all the RAF's air defence assets. The introduction of volunteer short service National Servicemen and the continuing level of volunteer reservists will allow for virtually all the point surface to air defence units to be manned, in time, by reservists. We also consider that the bulk of the airfield ground defence units will also be efficiently manned by reservists. This will allow for the maximum use to be made of the Royal Air Force Regiment Regulars to be deployed in Germany to secure the clutch airfields and to take over the manning of the Cruise missile units.

The efficiency of the existing reservists both individual and units have been recently tested (ex-Brave Defender, 1985). We are confident therefore that not only will the UK still be able to make use of the long term part-time volunteer for whom there will always be a place, but the reintroduction of a National Service scheme, which will be largely non-military, although recruits may volunteer for the military role, will be seen as an effective means of harnessing the youth of the country towards increasing their own security and that of their families.

Forward defence

The European mainland. The British Army of the Rhine has been, over the years, the visible sign of our commitment to the defence of the heartland of NATO. Its contribution of deterrence is that, by its presence in Germany, it has been, and still is, a political signal demonstrating to any would be aggressor that the United Kingdom will regard a military attack upon Western Germany as an attack upon herself. Thus it performs a deterrent role.

This deterrent role will be continued with the presence of a three brigade armoured division supported by an artillery division. Both these divisions will be manned entirely by Regulars and kept at war establishment. Thus the fire-power of these two formations, which we believe should be used directly under the operational command of Commander-in-Chief Central Region (CINCENT) as a hard-hitting mobile reserve, will have the fire-power at least equal to that of the Netherlands Corps, and greater than that of the Belgium Corps.

This reduction in ground force levels in the Central Region will be phased and will take a number of years. It will be vitally important that the visible increase in reinforcement capability to both Jutland and north Norway be seen to go hand in hand with the reduction of the British military contribution to the Central Front. We also believe that this change will be accompanied by a more complete strategic overhaul in the defence concept as at present practised in the Central Region.

RAF Germany. We intend to increase the strength of RAF Germany. This is, in part, to replace the loss of land forces with an increase in offensive strike/attack capability. The Harrier squadrons will remain and, with their ability to operate from dispersed sites, will continue to be an effective and relatively invulnerable force available to Commander Allied Air Forces Central Region (COMAAFCE). As the withdrawal of the two armoured divisions is near completion it is intended that the number of RAF fast jet squadrons stationed in Germany is increased from twelve to fourteen. To this end negotiations for a fifth airfield in Germany for the RAF will begin with the Federal Republic. In the late 1980s the arrival of the Harrier GR5 will improve our capability for offensive support. Like the Tornado, the aircraft will carry new weapons. An improved version of the BL 755 anti-armour weapon has entered service. At present it is for carriage on the Harrier GR3 and will subsequently be for the GR5. This will be superseded in the 1990s by a 'smart' anti-armour weapon.

The number of RAF Regiment squadrons stationed in Germany will be correspondingly increased as their auxiliary (reserve) units take on the air defence and grand security roles in the UK.

The Northern Region

Our reasons for changing our strategic defensive posture to concentrate more of our military power into this particular NATO area have already been adumbrated. We intend to reorganise 3 Commando Brigade and 5 Airborne Brigade together with the SAS Regiment into an assault division. This division will form a joint force headquarters for operations involving more than a single brigade task. It will further be responsible for planning, in conjunction with Flag Officer

Amphibious forces and with the appropriate RAF headquarters, for contingencies both within and outside the NATO area.

Specifically, contingencies will be planned for the landing of a two brigade task force in North Norway, the landing by air or sea or both of task forces of varying sizes on all the North Sea islands. This formation will also be responsible for contingency planning for the security of oil rigs in the North Sea.

As has already been mentioned further reinforcements to the Northern Region are also planned. The existing one infantry brigade with its logistics support contingency for operations in Denmark/ Jutland, will be increased to that of a three brigade division. A further second priority contingency for a two brigade division to land in South Norway is also intended in the long term. These contingencies are dependent upon the timetable of the withdrawal of the two armoured divisions from Germany.

Maritime tasks: the eastern Atlantic and Channel. Major objectives for any aggressor against the NATO Alliance could be the isolation of North Norway by denying the passage of outside reinforcements to the area, or (and) North Sea seaborne reinforcements and resupply. Such operations would take place in the event of a major aggression in the Central Region or in the North. It is, however, possible that whereas a major aggression in the Centre will be accompanied or preceded by military moves in the North, the same might not apply if military aggression took place in the North.[72]

'The United Kingdom provides 70 per cent of the forces involved'[73] in the defence of the Eastern Atlantic and the Channel. However, the new strategic emphasis which the Government now intends to place upon the Northern Region will require an increase in the strength of the Royal Navy in both submarines and surface ships. Again it is intended that, through the greater use at home of reservists and volunteer National Servicemen and women that more Regulars will thereby be released for sea duties. The Government also expects that, owing to the abandoning of the Trident programme, the skilled manpower thus released will enable a more balanced conventional navy to be built up. The Royal Air Force contributions will continue to be enhanced. The programme to convert the Nimrod maritime patrol aircraft to the improved MK2 standard has given a much better ASW capability to the fleet.

In the meantime a comprehensive study will be put in hand to see in what way the existing naval building programme will need to be modified in order that capabilities remain in line with the increased maritime responsibilities. It is expected that this review will show that there will have to be, over the next decade, a significant budgetary readjustment between the three services.

The reserves

'The simple most cost-effective way in which the front line capability of our regular forces can be augmented is by making the fullest possible use of our volunteer reserves.'[74] The experiences gained in exercises such as Brave Defender 1985 have confirmed this assessment. However, the introduction of National Service, even though the bulk of recruits will serve in the non-military role, will allow even greater use of Regulars in their prime role which will still remain as 'ex-UK' commitments.

The TA will have to undergo a radical reorganisation essentially forming two parts. One will carry out its traditional, and essential, military tasks and in future it is intended that the home based TA is melded much more closely into the Regular divisions on the basis that we have already discussed. The second role, in which it will be assisted in the provisions of training teams and Regular cadres, will be the civil defence role.

The Home Defence Force which was first raised in 1982 to provide static guard forces for lower priority key targets in time of tension or war will be absorbed into the military part of the TA.

The Royal Naval and Royal Marine reserves and the RAAF units will only take NS recruits who have volunteered to serve in that particular role.

Beyond the NATO area

As we have already stated neither NATO as an essentially maritime alliance nor the UK, an island nation, can ignore the strategic worldwide threat posed by the military power represented by the Soviet Navy nor the influence of political and economic factors generated by conflicting interests in all parts of the world. Furthermore, the UK still has residual interest in many parts of the globe, a result of history. There are treaty commitments which we would intend to honour if asked.

Garrisons

The Falklands garrisons of ships, aircraft and land forces provides a means of defending its British inhabitants. However, what is called the 'Fortress Falklands' syndrome justifies itself not on these grounds but upon the fact that, now we have a significant garrison on the Falklands, we can ensure that the surveillance of the South Atlantic, a need of extreme strategic importance to NATO, can become a reality. The Government intends therefore to develop the wherewithal in technical equipment and manpower to produce a surveillance facility which, because of the nature of the islands themselves, will be absolutely secure.

Hong Kong

The responsibility of Her Majesty's Government will end towards the end of the next decade. It is anticipated therefore that the defence responsibility for the colony will end at this time. This brings into question the future of the Gurkha battalions and other supporting units. That the links between the Gurkhas and the United Kingdom should come to an end is unthinkable. The Government intends therefore to enter into discussions with the Australian, New Zealand, Singapore and Malaysian Governments to see if there is a basis of maintaining this excellent force as Britain's contribution to the continued security of those states. We feel that it is possible that a British Gurkha base could be set up in the Northern Territory of Australia, where the Gurkhas can continue to train in jungle warfare. It is thought that, if the brigade was to have this situation it would be formally under the operational control of the Australian Government although still part of the British order of battle. It would have a continuing and important role in helping to maintain the security of those Commonwealth States. This is a long term problem and there will be no intention of attempting to reach any hasty decision on the matter.

Forces flexibility

The creation of an assault division with its headquarters forming a joint field force HQ, together with the improved amphibious and air transport capabilities, is intended to be a part of Britain's increased contribution to the NATO Northern Region. At the same time it will give the UK a much improved capability to assist allies outside the NATO area if the need should arise.

Notes

1. This definition has been taken, almost word for word, from J. I. Coffey, *Arms Control and European Security* (London: Chatto & Windus, 1977) p. 22.
2. Taken from the Atlantic Council of the United States Policy Paper, *Arms Control* (Washington DC: Int. Economic Studies Inst., March 1983) pp. 67–70.
3. The author was a lecturer at the JWE, 1975–7.
4. *The Military Balance 1982–3*, International Institute for Strategic Studies. London. pp. 112–15.
5. Robert J. Hawks USN (Retd), Inst. for Foreign Policy Analysis, Inc., Aug. 1980.
6. Richard Humble, *Aircraft Carriers* (London: Michael Joseph, 1982), ch. 9, 'The Soviet Menace', p. 174.
7. Omega Report (Adam Smith Inst., 1983) p. 11.
8. Dr Marion K. Leighton, 'The Soviet Threat to NATO's Northern Flank' Nat. Strategy Information Centre Inc., NY, Agenda Paper No. 10, 1979, p. 3.
9. 'Royal Navy's Urgent Priorities', *Spectator*, 8 June 1974, p. 697.
10. Leighton, 'Soviet Threat to NATO's Northern Flank', p. 7.
11. Ibid., p. 30.
12. *The Times*, 11 Mar. 1978.
13. *Security and Arms Control: The Search for a More Stable Peace* (Washington DC: US Dept of State, June 1983) p. 27.
14. Sir James Cable, 'Surprise and the Simple Scenario', *RUSI Journal*, vol. 128, no. 1 (March, 1983) p. 34.
15. Leighton, 'Soviet Threat to NATO's Northern Flank', p. 87.
16. For further reading on this subject see Manfried Hamm, *Chemical Warfare, The Growing Threat to Europe* (Inst. for European Defence and Strategic Studies, 1984).
17. *Report of the European Security Study*, ESECS (Macmillan, 1983).
18. Henry A. Kissinger, *The Troubled Partnership* (McGraw-Hill, 1965) p. 96.
19. Ibid., p. 97.
20. Ibid., p. 25.
21. McNamara, Address before the Fellows of the American Bar Foundation, Chicago, Illinois, 17 Feb. 1962.
22. Kissinger, *The Troubled Partnership*, p. 113.
23. 'Political Will and the Flexible Response', *Spectator*, 25 May 1974.
24. *Spectator*, 24 May 1974.
25. Speech appeared in *RUSI Journal* (Sept. 1982) p. 12.
26. Ibid., p. 14.
27. Complete text, *RUSI Journal* (Dec. 1982) pp. 21–5.
28. Complete text, *RUSI Journal* (Sept. 1982) p. 12.
29. Omega Report (Adam Smith Inst., 1983) p. 4.

30. Kevin Harrison, 'From Independence to Dependence', *RUSI Journal*, Dec. 1982.
31. Ibid.
32. 'Trojan Peace: Some Deterrent Propositions Tested', Theresa A. Smith Graduate School of International Studies, Denver, 1982, p. xi.
33. R. Speed, *Strategic Deterrence in the 1980s* (Stamford: Hoover Institution, 1979) p. 7.
34. Wilfried Hofman, 'Is NATO's Defence Policy Facing a Crisis?', *NATO Review*, Aug. 1984.
35. Michael Mandelbaum, *The Nuclear Question: The United States and Nuclear Weapons, 1946–76* (Cambridge Univ. Press, 1979) p. 58.
36. J. I. Coffey, *Arms Control and European Security*. Studies in Intr. Security. Published for ISSC (London: Chatto & Windus, 1979) p. 84.
37. 'Arms Control, East–West Relations and the Atlantic Alliance. Closing the Gaps'. Atlantic Council Working Group on Arms Control (Washington, DC, Mar. 1983).
38. 'Arms Control, East/West Relations', Atlantic Council Policy Paper (Mar. 1983) p. 38.
39. See, for example, Laurence Martin, *Arms and Strategy: An International Survey of Modern Defence* (London: Weidenfeld & Nicolson, 1973).
40. Donald D. Maclean, *British Foreign Policy Since Suez 1956–68* (London: Hodder & Stoughton, 1970) p. 25.
41. 'From Independence to Dependence', *RUSI Journal* (Dec. 1982) p. 26.
42. *Guardian*, 20 April 1960.
43. David Numerby, *President Kennedy and Britain* (London: Bodley Head, 1972) p. 117.
44. Kissinger, *The Troubled Partnership*, p. 81.
45. Ibid., p. 81.
46. *RUSI Journal* (Dec. 1982) p. 29.
47. *Statement on Defence Estimates, 1981*, pt I (London: HMSO) p. 14.
48. Ibid., p. 13.
49. Ibid., para. 209.
50. *Emergency Planning Guidance to Local Authorities* (issued by Home Office).
51. Major-General Tar Rolf Bryntensen, 'Norway's Civil Emergency Planning', *NATO Review*, June 1985.
52. Ibid.
53. Ibid.
54. Omega Report, 1983, p. 36, para. 1.
55. Ibid., p. 36, para. 2.
56. Ibid., p. 27, para. 2 (original source: 'The Military Balance').
57. Defence White Paper, 1985, pt II, p. 6.
58. Ibid., p. 24, paras 430–1.
59. *Ships and Aircraft of the US Fleet*, 13th ed. (Arms and Armor Press, 1985) p. 214.
60. Defence White Paper, 1985, pt I, p. 30, paras 458–60.
61. Omega Report, 1983, p. 52.
62. Defence White Paper, 1984, pt I, p. 1.
63. Ibid., para. 102.

64. Ibid., para. 103.
65. Ibid., para. 103.
66. For further reading, *NATO's Strategy: A Case of Outdated Priorities*, Inst. for European Defence and Strategic Studies Paper No. 11.
67. See General Sven Hauge, 'Defence Probably Better Than Ever but Weaker Relative to Threat', *Norwegian Defence Review, 1983–84*.
68. Defence White Paper, 1984, pt I, para. 130.
69. Ibid., para. 402.
70. Chs 6 and 7.
71. Defence White Paper, 1984, pt I, para. 407.
72. *NATO's Strategy: A Case of Outdated Priorities*, p. 20.
73. Defence White Paper, 1984, pt I, para. 429.
74. Ibid., para. 440.

Index